Navigating the Waves of Change

Navigating the Waves of Change
CHANGE IS CONSTANT IN A DYNAMIC CHURCH

David Biser

WestBow
PRESS®
A DIVISION OF THOMAS NELSON
& ZONDERVAN

WestBow Press books may be ordered through booksellers or by contacting:

WestBow Press
A Division of Thomas Nelson & Zondervan
1663 Liberty Drive
Bloomington, IN 47403
www.westbowpress.com
1 (866) 928-1240

THE HOLY BIBLE, NEW INTERNATIONAL VERSION®, NIV® Copyright © 1973, 1978, 1984, 2011 by Biblica, Inc.® Used by permission. All rights reserved worldwide.

ISBN: 978-1-5127-6930-2 (sc)
ISBN: 978-1-5127-6931-9 (hc)
ISBN: 978-1-5127-6929-6 (e)

Library of Congress Control Number: 2016920865

Print information available on the last page.

WestBow Press rev. date: 12/27/2016

Contents

Acknowledgement

Writing a book is never a singular adventure taken on by one person. Every person in the life of a writer is a part of the story or the book in some way. So, if you are a part of my family, my community, my denomination, my local congregation, or my friendship circle…thank you! You had a big part in making this book a reality. You may have been a part of the process of transformation the church went through that you will read about. You may have been a part of a conversation that sparked an idea or area of the book that needed written. If you are one of the members of the congregation or staff, God bless you. You lived through a difficult season in the life of this church and we survived. If you are one of the monks at Mount Saviour monastery in New York, your quiet place of refuge gave me a beautiful place to connect with the Divine, to be spiritually filled and to write.

If you are one of the trusted people who edited this work, you took what I wrote and made sense of it. If you are one of my children, there were times when you gave more than was required so that I could give what was needed to the church I pastored through all of this change. And especially, if you're my wife, you gave long sleepless nights, tears, laughter, support, a sounding board, and love that saw me through as Jesus lives in and through you.

Thank you all…for letting me finally tell our story.

Introduction

They were not at all ready. For that matter, neither was I – no one was, except God who seems always ready for change and yet compassionate about waiting for us to catch up. It was 2005 and my friend and I were returning from one of those meetings that people in mainline denominations "have" to attend from time-to-time. We had done our duty; we went, we endured as much as we could, and we left. We didn't enjoy it and we had not paid much attention. Instead, as usual when we found ourselves in one of these situations, we had spent much of the time talking about the future. His future, my future, the future of the church we were pastoring together: he the lead pastor and me the associate pastor. Much of the conversation focused on what it was we were going to do in the immediate future. We both knew we felt an urging from God to go to a whole new level.

Paul, my friend, was talking about planting a church as the next thing we would do. He would provide the pastoral anchor for the current congregation and I would soar into a new world of church planting. We talked about our gifts, our current roles and how they would change if we went down this path. We talked about our concern for our mainline denomination (United Methodist) and its inability to successfully launch or plant new churches. Our own area, central Pennsylvania, had experienced very few successful launches in all the time my friend could remember, and that was over 25 years.

We knew that our next adventure together was planting a church. We both felt it deep down in our guts. So, now what? We left the gathering early and on our drive home we pulled the car over on a stretch of road that was experiencing a huge amount of transition. We both felt God speaking to us as we drove down the road that was previously surrounded by farmland and was now being developed into 2000+ homes over the next five years. We stopped. I forget who was driving. What I do remember is standing beside Paul on the side of the road and talking about receiving the answer to the "what now" question we had been asking. For God, the "what now" question was answered with "HERE, PLANT HERE!" We were not ready for such a speedy confirmation or such a clear answer to a question asked only moments before. In hind sight, God was moving quickly that day and would do so for years to follow. As we went through this wild adventure, and as we live it out today, we know that God is on the move and continues to call us to more and more. Even though we are not always ready, God is still moving, with us, without us, and sometimes in spite of us.

The journey from a mainline denominational church to one church with four locations and seven services each weekend, and with 600 in attendance each week, has been an incredible ride. It is my plan to share some of the things we've done and gone through so that you don't have to create the wheel yourself. In effect, we cut a path but, you get the benefit of traveling that path that has already been cut. You may look at the things in this book and think that it is impossible. But, remember, Jesus said that all things are possible. I will also say that there is a New Testament process for launching a new thing. This journey must start with prayer and fasting. God must be

> Jesus looked at them and said, "With man this is impossible, but not with God; all things are possible with God.
> Mark 10:27 NIV.

at the beginning of everything or the process will wear you out. This has not been an easy road, but I have never wanted to throw in the towel or turn back. It has given me and several other members of our staff some serious family and medical issues to deal with. There is great evil lurking when good men and women strive to do what seems like the impossible with God.

Much, if not all, that you will read is a spiritual tale. All of it includes prayer, fasting, retreats, long days and even longer nights, countless meetings, and endless struggles. While this journey is hard, remember in the words of Rick Warren as he started off The Purpose Driven Life: "It's not about you." If you are willing to sacrifice it *all* in order to gain everything, keep reading. If the thought of sixty to seventy hour weeks, walks through fields with real estate agents and developers, negotiations with school district boards over leasing space, long talks with the overseers in your life (in my case it's a district superintendent and bishop) are all scary to you – I will warn you, that's just the tip of the iceberg. People will leave your fold, they will call you names, they will find a different exit door on Sunday mornings to avoid shaking hands with you, and co-workers in the kingdom will watch to see if you can swim in the deep end or whether you're going to foolishly drown. This is going to hurt. If that scares you, close the cover and put this book far away from where you are and go back to God to see what He wants you to do next because this is not it.

Now, if you are still reading it's probably because you have lived long enough, believed long enough, or are just foolish enough to think God can do anything. You also believe that God wants to use you to do something completely out of your control with your life and ministry. For those still reading, I want to take a moment to say that, as challenging and scary as it was to move from mainline to multi-site, it has been ten times more rewarding. My worst days, and there have been a few, were far better than I ever dreamed my life could be. I still pinch myself in disbelief. I get to do this job everyday! Wow! God has set aside this task and created me especially for this adventure.

Unbelievable! I get to be one of the pastors who works with four sites, multiple venues, and awesome staff, kids, youth, small groups, old and young, missions, straight and gay, two weeks clean and sober, suffering from divorce or fifty plus years married, and the list goes on. I love my job, my calling, my life. Why, because we're multi-site? Because I am a pastor? No – because I have discovered that obedience to God brings a joy that cannot be matched. I do not need anything in this world to make me happy. My happiness is in pleasing God. Now, I will admit, it helps when there is evidence that God is at work in the things we are doing. It is fantastic when people move into deep places in their spiritual life and God starts changing the personal and corporate atmosphere of the people you lead. Because of that I choose to give all my days in service to God. In return, for no other reason than an amazing love, God chooses to give me the desires of my heart. I didn't think it could get better. It has and I wasn't ready for that...none of us were. But, it's been the ride of my life and I would not trade it for anything.

Chapter 1
Surviving the Change

Every church gets an opportunity handed to it from time to time and if the leaders have their eyes open they will catch the waves God sends and ride them to wherever God is taking them. Some churches see the wave coming and like new comers on the beach they either run and try not to get blasted or they honker down and try to withstand the blow. Occasionally there are those who are oblivious to the waves. They are not paying attention and they get plowed over. Videos of these moments often end up on Facebook. I have friends who have seen the wave of opportunity heading their way. Some took the "run-away" mentality and others employed the honker down method. I have been fortunate to be just bold enough to believe God is so sufficient in all I need that when waves are coming, I have chosen a third option. I tend to run for the wave, dive in head first, and let it pound my body so that I can experience the full fury of the power of the Almighty God we serve.

I like the waves...I am a bit of an adrenaline junkie. Over the last few years I have white water rafted with groups of teens and adults, I have tandem parachuted at 14,000 feet, I have rock climbed, bungee jumped, and especially like catapulting rollercoaster's – you know, the ones that go from zero to sixty miles per hour in just a few seconds. My favorite ride at Walt Disney World, Hollywood Studios is The Rockin' Roller Coaster. So, it should come as no surprise that when waves start building out at sea I start heading out into the water. I share that to give you a bit of insight into the kind of person I am. I am always looking for a new opportunity and I see adventure in every thing that can take me and the church to a whole new level. I enjoy a challenge and I love change.

Now, I know that kind of adventurous spirit is not, well let's use the word "normal." So, if the idea of leading change makes you nauseous, you are not alone. According to some of the statistics I have seen, most pastors are introverts who not only do not like conflict, they tend to be conflict avoiders. And there are times that as a pastor, it is like we are inflicting change on people instead of leading them through it. So, if change is staring you in the face and seems way too scary, there are two things I would like to recommend...pray and take long, deep, cleansing breaths. Change is not easy and it must be surrounded with prayer and a sense that God is the one who is ultimately going to make the needed changes happen at your church. Being a person of prayer and remaining a calming presence in your congregation is vitally important. It will see you through when challenges get overwhelming and the wave seems too big to manage.

When a huge challenge came our way a few years ago, my first reaction was to drop to my knees and pray. The trial put me in a hurting place personally but I also knew that God was calling me to a new life. A wave was building and getting ready to crash. I had not seen this wave coming and when it hit it sent me tumbling around in the violent surf as it crashed into my life. My mind and body were being tossed around by an incredible experience. My prayer was, "Oh God, let me do this well. Let me do things in a way that will bring glory and honor to you. I know you are in this God, so give me all I need to do this well." God heard my prayer that day, a day when major crisis came into my life and the life of the church.

Today, CrossPoint is a growing congregation of 600 members with just around 600 average attenders at seven services each week at four locations in the greater Harrisburg, Pennsylvania area. But, let me back up a bit and talk about the wave that God sent. In 2004 the senior pastor and I began talking about the future. The congregation was growing and people were starting to chomp at the bit asking about what was next. To get to a place where people were excited about the future we had done an extensive amount of work in the area of leadership via the teachings of guys like Bill Easum, Tom Bandy, John Maxwell, and Bill Hybels. We were a part of the pilot project when Rick Warren and Saddleback Church launched the Purpose Driven Church as a nationwide project. We piloted Purpose Driven Life and 40 Days of Purpose as well. Those congregation wide studies opened people to the never-ending challenge of God to be a part of the Kingdom building process. Now, our leaders were looking for a new place to go and implement everything they had been learning.

The senior pastor was not only great leader but, was also my best friend. We did things together at the church and outside the church. We really enjoyed being with each other, which can be rare among lead and associate pastors. He got to the church just one year before I got there and he laid the ground work for the associate pastor position that I was to fill. During our years working together we met on purpose at least once a week. We also met at those times when things came up that we needed to talk about or work through together. So, as we sensed the wave that was swelling, we began to talk more and more. One day, Paul (Paul Lauchle) and I were at one of those one-day trainings that everyone must attend when you're a part of a mainline denomination. We had both gotten the letter that stated clearly that our attendance was required.

So, we attended as much as we could and then we ducked out early. While we were at the training we sat in the back and talked about an idea we both had bouncing around in our heads...planting a church. We felt that was to be the next thing for us to do. Leaders from the current church campus would go out and seed a new congregation. It was an adventure and we were both getting excited about it. It would mean once again that the congregation would need to face change but, Paul was confident that we could lead everyone through it. We had done it before.

A few years earlier we moved from two services on Sunday

morning and one service on Saturday evenings to three services on Sunday morning. I led the Saturday evening service and we believed that if it was going to grow it would need to move to Sunday morning. That meant that I would no longer be a part of our traditional worship services on Sunday mornings and that I would be leading a new, contemporary service in the all-purpose room. The congregation did not like seeing us separated, we had great chemistry, but we did not give them a choice. We claimed the Great Commandment and the Great Commission as our reason for starting this new service on Sunday morning and shutting down the Saturday evening service.

As Paul and I left that training event (okay, ducked out early) we began the drive back to the church talking about the church plant idea. We entered a corridor of land that was being churned over by huge pieces of machinery. Every where we looked we saw the evidence of new beginnings. We had heard in the news that most of the land on this several mile corridor had been sold and was being developed. We could not believe how extensive it was when we saw it. We pulled over to get a better look at all that was going on and to talk some more.

As we stood by the car on the side of the road we realized that we had found the area God was calling us to. This newly developing area was soon to see thousands of new homes and there were very few churches. We looked at each other and asked, "are you thinking what I'm thinking?" Whenever you and someone close to you in ministry asks that question of each other at the same time, watch out. That kind of questioning can be the words that are the precursor to a huge wave, get ready to ride. God just might be ready to pull the rug out from underneath you. Your personal and professional comfort and stability may very well be in jeopardy.

We got back in the car and drove back to the church. In the months following we began sharing the dream with others. Paul and I talked about what our leadership would look like. As the vision developed, Paul kept challenging me to consider being the one to launch the new church. I was the youth pastor and the teaching pastor for our contemporary service. I had always thought that I would be a "youth pastor guy" all my life. I did not want to lead a church, not me. I got my passion fulfilled by hanging out with middle school, high school and college students, going on retreats, spending summers at the Creation Festival and camp outs, and rocking out to contemporary music. Our contemporary service was our fastest growing service and I loved it. The new plant was going to be contemporary as well and Paul was pushing me to make the decision to lead it. Just like him, I would lead two services: the current contemporary service at our first site and the new one at the plant as well.

Then we learned about a new idea taking shape in the Christian world, multi-site church. In 2005 we attended a one-day seminar held by the great people out at Community Christian Church in the greater Chicago area. Community Christian had six locations at the time and were working on the plans for number seven. The workshop walked our staff through the evaluation steps so that we could consider whether multi-site was for us, whether we were ready, and what things we needed to do next. The workshop was led by Dave Ferguson, Pat Masek, Jon Ferguson and Eric Bramlett. These are the same people who now lead the NewThing Network and the Exponential Conference and Exponential Network. They walked us through the seven things that needed to be in place that they had established as vital to success. We spent the day working well as a team and really feeding off their leadership. By the end of the day we had discovered that we had six of the seven steps in place. Those seven things are:

1. God's calling to launch
2. A vision
3. A campus pastor/leader
4. Staff and board support
5. A missional mindset
6. Finances
7. Location

The only thing missing from our plan was a location. So, when we returned we knew what we were going to be doing, we just didn't know where - so our next task was to find a location.

We began the search in very traditional ways. Real estate people were contacted within the congregation who could start looking for a place. We did not have tons of money, but we had positive leadership and the support of a strong congregation. We were not afraid to go into debt because we had a high level of confidence and momentum. We began an extensive search in the corridor of land we had tagged as our target area. The area is 8 miles from our first location and, more importantly, a community that orients itself in different areas than the majority of attenders at the first campus. The problem was that the area was being developed from farm land to housing developments and townhouse communities. There were no existing buildings or structures that we could move into and start a campus. We looked at an old greenhouse that needed a huge amount of work and was not big enough nor had enough parking. We would have paid a million dollars for a fixer-upper on just 6 acres. We walked away from that deal shaking our heads and wondering what God was up to because nothing was showing itself to be the place for us to launch.

Then, in July of 2006, Paul and I walked into the South Hanover Elementary School. This is a small school that services the corridor we had been talking about. It is well established and everyone knows its location even though it is a bit off the beaten path. The school district had done some renovations to the school including a new all- purpose gym/auditorium/cafeteria. We walked in and were blown away. The room was almost identical to the all-purpose room at our current campus. We toured the building and began dreaming: classrooms here, child care over there, children's worship in this space, and so on. Everything was clean and well kept. The lighting was great, lots of windows and open hallways. The principle at the school was wonderful. She was inviting and welcoming. We talked about what we wanted to do and we shared the vision with her and watched as she got excited with us about what God was going to do in this community. She attended a local mainline church and was thrilled to see some new blood come to town. We had found our location! Now we needed to convince others to catch the vision of the future of our church.

Paul had been on a 40-day study leave where he had read a bunch of books, checked out other churches, met with leaders and spent time with God. The result was the rough draft of a new vision and direction for the church that would include multi-site. I left for a mission trip with our high school youth ministry. I was going to be in the most challenging area of Orlando, Florida where poverty, drugs, language barriers and shattered dreams were trashing lives. I would be spending the next week working at a church school; hanging drywall, fixing doors, laying tile, replacing carpeting and doing general repairs with our student ministry. It was going to be a great time. There were lots of things that needed done. The leaders had set a calendar that included scheduled times of taking the rough draft and chiseling it down into a final form that would be presented to the church by the end of the year and implemented in January of 2007.

Just as everything seemed to be coming together so well, a huge, unexpected and tragic thing happened. My friend and lead pastor, Paul, was out one evening and had pulled over along the side of the road. They found him the next morning. He had finished his physical life's journey there on the side of the road because of a pulmonary embolism. I got the call while I was still on the mission trip in Florida. It was Friday morning; I remember it like it was yesterday. I was told to sit down because this was going to be very tough news. I ended up on my knees asking God to make something good happen from this and I prayed that I could do well those things that would be needed of me. Paul was gone; now what? The decision was easy...we go on. We take the vision, finalize it and do exactly what God had in store for us as leaders and as a church.

I cannot imagine anything more catastrophic than the sudden death of the lead pastor of a church poised to ride a God-sent wave. Here one day, gone the next at 55 years of age. Completely unexpected, a total shock. The effect was deep and wide. Over 1000 people attended his memorial service. Local television channels covered it. He was very well known and loved. I was in shock and yet, I was now, by default, the lead pastor of a church on the move.

I wish I would have known then what I know now. What I knew was that my best friend was gone. What I knew was that there was a grieving family at the church parsonage that I needed to get home to. What I knew was that there would be a congregation that was going to have their world rocked. What I did not know was just how deeply his death would affect everything we did and everything I am. We were just not ready for the crash of this wave to our church and our lives.

There will be a few times during this book that I will say clearly that if I could go back and do things differently, I would. One of those times is right here. I was in no shape to care for a congregation let alone move a vision forward. In hind sight, I know now that I should have taken three months off to process, grieve and make sure I was ready. Instead, I postponed my own grieving and dove into my work, which I've learned since then, is a form of grieving itself.

> There will be a few times during this book that I will say clearly that if I could go back and do things differently, I would.

It would take me years to process what had happened. There were theological things that I needed to wrestle with. There was the pain of losing a friend, mentor and buddy. There was the congregation, who needed a pastor instead of a task master (which I became from time to time). I lost some of my pastoral sympathy during those years and found myself saying things like: if I can do it, they should be able to do it too. I assumed that since I was so very close to the situation and I could put my feelings on the back burner and focus on the vision God had given us that other people, who were not as close to him as I was, should be able to buck up. I still shake my head when I think about how insensitive I was during those days, weeks, months and years. If you were there and I hurt you, I apologize…I should have known better and let me tell you, I know better now. I like to think that I'm a better leader today than I was then.

God had forced our hand and God had more in store for us to come than we could imagine. This was a huge wave smashing into our church. But, God can take the catastrophic and make the miraculous happen. God can take our worst and make it His best. And that's exactly what God was going to do next. God had given us a vision and while the man God used to give us the vision was gone; the vision did not go with him. So, let's look at what happened next and how the vision came to life.

Reflection Questions:

+   What significant events inside your church or out in your community have happened that could be the catalyst for the change God is calling you to accomplish?
+   What change have you or the congregation navigated before? How did it go? What concerns you the most about future changes?
+   How do you tend to face the challenges and changes that life throws at you?
+   Look at the seven things that need to be in place before you can move forward. Do you have all seven? If not, what will you need to do to get there?

Chapter 2
Crafting the Vision

The waves of change began to churn and develop years before they actually came to the surface and landed on the beach. The vision for CrossPoint Church was put into place in 1997, a full nine years before the changes would be implemented. The vision included sweeping and systemic changes that would see the church into the future. This vision came out of the *Purpose Driven Church* movement that was beginning to take hold in the United States. We were able to take some of the "permission giving" revisions that the United Methodist denomination had instituted and use them to build a new leadership structure. The United Methodist Church had opened the door and had given local congregations a fair amount of autonomy in how it arranges such things as boards and committees. So, in light of the positive things found in being Purpose Driven, a time of restructuring was instituted that would make us more streamlined and effective.

> "We did not get where we are without fundamental changes to our structures and thought processes about how ministry gets accomplished."

I cannot stress enough how important it was that we laid this ground work first. We did not get where we are without fundamental changes to our structures and thought processes about how ministry gets accomplished. We were expecting big things and that meant changes that would make way to providing systems for a new look.

The epitome of insanity is doing the same thing over and over and expecting different results (modified version of Albert Einstein's quote). There was no way for real growth to happen while doing the same thing we've always done in the very same ways. There needed to be a change. And as difficult as it is to make change happen in a church, doing things the same way it was done twenty, thirty, forty, or more years ago just will not work in our current culture.

In 1996 our church did away with the traditional denominational look of an administrative board that included too many people for decisions to be accomplished (well over 50-60 at each monthly meeting). It was a monthly exercise in building an elephant by committee. Very little gets done at most churches under this archaic system of committees and large boards. It has been said that committees, by their very nature, accomplish very little. The very idea that a large group of people coming from every possible walk in life and spiritual journey will be able to lead a church in the right direction is as foreign to success as putting athletes from different disciplines onto one team and expecting a win. On the other hand, given a united vision, people can join together for the sole purpose of experiencing success through joining strengths and gifts. We promote the body of Christ (1 Corinthians 12) understanding of who we are and how we function together as a church. This tenet of scripture can separate those churches who just function from week to week from those churches who reach people and grow. Check out Marcus Buckingham's "Go Put Your Strengths To Work" for more on this idea.

At CrossPoint Church we have done away with every committee except those we are required by our denomination (and for good reason) to maintain. They are: Church Council (some would call this an elders board), Staff/Parish Relations Committee (this might be the deacons board at a lot of churches) and Trustees. We also made a change to the common terminology around the church. We decided that ministries happen via teams (not committees) so we removed the word "committee" from everything we do and moved to the word "team" instead. We believe teams get things done, committees kill things and often it is a long, agonizing death. So, at CrossPoint Church there is a Vacation Bible School Team, Hospitality Teams, a Eucharistic Ministry Team, Meal Ministry Team, worship teams, launch teams and more. We find that teams allow for focus and foster unity. The word "committee" has become a swear word for us and we have effectively removed the word completely from our vocabulary.

First Things First

One of the first things a leader who wants to see a God-ordained change needs to do is to evaluate the structures that exist, determine where they are leading you and your church, and begin a game plan for change. Moving from outdated and spiritless committees to teams with purpose and authority is one of the key reasons we were able to make the changes we did make. But, this takes strength as a leader. There will be times when you will feel timid or think that the old things aren't too broken so why fix them. Let me remind you, if the old things were working you would not be reading this book. There are times when change comes around the corner and blindsides us and it is extremely important to be ready. Culture can introduce change, a denominational move in one direction or another can cause change, a pastoral move can bring change. Whatever causes the change, no matter what the size of the change might be, leaders will need to be ready to act and react.

> Let me remind you, if the old things were working you would not be reading this book.

There are other times when, as a leader, you need to force change if anything new or any significant growth is going to happen. Sitting back and doing the same old things that you've always done or your denomination has always done will not get you or the church to the place God wants you. God is a fluid, dynamic God who is unchanging and yet, causing change in us, our systems, our structures and our denominations every single day in order to touch the generation your church is called to reach. The bold leader who is willing to venture off of the comfortable shores and dive into the waves will see remarkable results.

This is a leadership issue for you and the Church. The Church of Jesus Christ does not need more status quo leaders or managers. Whether it's the "do things like usual" pastor or the "we've never done it that way" member, God is calling for a change. We can all see where not changing has gotten us…huge national decline in attendance and sloppy theology where the majority of Christ followers believe that there may be more than one way to heaven – ways other than Jesus Christ as the only Son of God who died and rose again to redeem the world. Currently, over 3000 churches are closing every year (LifeWay statistics).

Is it any wonder when most churches refuse to consider the ramifications of doing what we did yesterday hoping it will work tomorrow? Every aspect of the church you lead or are a part of should be up for evaluation. Long ago we decided that there are no "sacred cows" that can't be evaluated and subsequently changed. We also declared that there are no "sacred spaces" any more. The senior adult classroom can also serve as the conference room. The office can also be a small group gathering place. The all-purpose room can be a worship center. Evaluation helps everyone understand that what we do is so important that we are going to ask if what we are actually doing matters and/or should be happening. Ouch, right?

The next thing you will probably need to do is go back to school. By that I mean each leader needs to dive into a time of learning. I spend a great deal of time listening to other great leaders. John Maxwell is one of my favorites along with Bill Hybels, Tom Bandy, Thom Rainer, Andy Stanley, George Hunter, Rick Warren, Bill Easum, Lyle Schaller, Carey Nieuwhof, and Ed Young just to name a few. Someday I would like to meet each one of them in person. My office is filled with their books. I listen to their pod casts when I am out walking or mowing the lawn. Leaders get great direction from other leaders. God uses them to sharpen us and build us up. If you're not listening to or reading other great leaders, then don't think that anything extraordinary is going to happen. Yes, God can do miracles, but I believe that we need to be reaching out and learning from those God is already blessing in the Kingdom.

> As iron sharpens iron, so
> one man sharpens another.
> Proverbs 27:17 NIV

If you are the pastor, you have probably discovered that they did not teach you everything you needed to know about leading a church when you were in seminary. A master of divinity does not give you what you need to know to make change happen.

The first vision from 1997 challenged the church into a total restructuring. We moved from a board/pastor led church to a staff led church. We changed things like our understanding of membership by creating a hybrid version of *The Purpose Driven Church* baseball diamond. Our vision began to move us onto position that would be realized about 10 years later. That vision from 1997 lasted for five years and at the end of five years we made a mistake that we noticed only in retrospect. We moved into a new five-year vision that was for all intent and purposes all about keeping the things of the first vision going as they were. We even called it *Keep the Candle Burning* the candle being the first five-year vision.

The idea was that all the things that we did in the first five years were working well so, let's keep doing them. The church was growing, we had more programs than you could shake a stick at (that's not a good thing by the way, read *Simple Church*, Rainer/Geiger) and we were really, really, busy. We took a balky mission statement and reduced it to just a few words; *Know, Love, Serve and Share Jesus*. We were moving fast and great things were happening but, we were not looking ahead at what was coming and we were not considering new leadership models for where we were heading, for the anticipated growth. We were moving straight toward a plateau and we were not making the appropriate changes to prevent it.

In 2004 we peaked as a congregation of 700 members with an average attendance of 632 in weekly worship at three services in one campus. In 2005 we began seeing a plateau and in the beginning of

2006 we started seeing decline. The plateau in '05 facilitated the move toward launching a church and eventually going multi-site. The *Keep the Candle Burning* vision had expired at the end of 2005 and we went into 2006 visionless. The resulting decline in '06 pushed our staff into conversations about our future and the need for a new vision. We went on a staff retreat to talk about it, we traveled to the National Church Planters Conference in April 2006 where we got some great encouragement. Our staff sat around tables and on patios, at lunches and dinners talking about it with each other.

The decline and lack of vision sent our lead pastor (Paul) into the 40-day study leave where he pulled from a huge amount of resources and a lot of time alone with God to craft a rough draft of our Dream 20/20. We truly felt like we were on our way. We felt the leadership of God moving us in a new direction that would take us to a new place. All we needed to do was bring the vision from draft form to its final form and launch it in 2007. It would be the vision that would take us to the year 20/20 and give us clarity and focus.

We knew God was doing something remarkable. We did not know just how big it would be. But, real change is systemic and can often feel catastrophic to the body. Like an antibiotic that affects the entire body, God often causes change that is full and complete because any remnant of the old thing can come back to cause problems later. God did this kind of thing repeatedly in the Old Testament. Rules that required the Hebrew people to stay separated from foreigners, to kill every one of an opposing tribe or people, get rid of all the yeast in the house, etc. From time to time God cleans house. Mike Slaughter talks about his start at Ginghamsburg Church in Tipp City, Ohio and how he grew the church down to almost nothing before it could grow up to where it's at today, a thriving congregation of over 4000 in worship each weekend.

When catastrophic change hits, you can make the choice to 1) curl up into a ball or 2) take the challenge and ride the wave. (That's assuming you were watching and were not taken unawares by the wave). For CrossPoint Church the tidal wave that hit us was the death of the lead pastor. The staff made the decision to take the ride and what a ride it's been. We could not do it alone. I knew that. It would take a great deal of help. A retired pastor was assigned who gave great help and offered insight gained from years of valuable servant leadership. We sought out consultants. We used every available resource that we could plug into. Community Christian Church has been instrumental in helping us. We also drew on the wisdom of places like Sea Coast and North Point – both multi-site churches, as well as Leadership Network, Leadership Summit, the Exponential Church Conference, and others who were ahead of us in multi-site and church growth via discipleship building.

The most important thing we did was contract with an active participant within the congregation, Steve Clay. Steve is one of the partners at Momentum Inc., a company that helps major corporations evaluate, streamline, reorganize, and move their company forward. Steve has been working with Fortune 500 companies as well as state government and military operations. Steve has the unique ability to see what is going on, to analyze the data, and give powerful advice. He also has the ability to see the project along the way. I will talk more about Steve and the other people we learned to lean on during our time of formulating the mission and vision for CrossPoint Church in chapter 3 *What the Vision Requires*. For now, let me show you what Steve showed us that was such a huge help.

Most organizations have it all backwards. Their mission statement is really their vision and their vision statement is really their mission. We had it backwards and now I see how many other churches have it backwards as well. The truth is, the church's mission is the unchanging purpose of your particular congregation, at its particular location. It will hardly ever change and if it does it is because something major happens that forces the mission to change such as a change in the demographics of the surrounding area or the church moves from its current place of ministry to another location. The mission is the timeless call of God upon a congregation. Each congregation has a different mission.

The Importance of Mission

Two churches can be right down the street from each other and both are thriving because they both recognize their mission. The mission is why we exist. It is the reason you are where you are for just such a time as this. When all the external things are stripped away, this is what is left. It's not a program, an event, a picture of what you want, but who you are at the very core of your being as a congregation. It should not change drastically with the changing of pastoral leadership because the pastor is not the one who is given the solitary responsibility of carrying out the mission…it belongs to everyone in the congregation/organization. Pastors come and go, the mission does not change that easily. It is basic and simple. It is based on scripture (because God does not ask a church to do what He has not already commanded in the Word for us to accomplish). The mission needs to fit on a t-shirt and must be easy to remember and easy to follow. If you need to explain it or define it, for people to understand it, it's not going to work.

The mission of CrossPoint Church is *Love God, Love Others and Make Disciples*. That's what we do…it's who we are. When everything else is gone that is what is left. It is the mission of our church to do those three things. Anything else causes loss of focus and gets us off course. We use our vision to guide and direct who we are and what we do. We also use it to help people to understand the Gospel, the Good News of Jesus. The very basic desire of God in our lives is that we learn to love God with all our heart, all our soul and all our mind. We do that as we worship God each weekend at our six celebration services. We are called to love our neighbor as ourselves. That's the *Love Others* part.

We do that by plugging into small groups where we nurture and care for others as we learn and grow. Sound like the Great Commandment? You're right, it is. Matthew 22:37 (NIV): **Love the Lord your God with all your heart and with all your soul and with all your mind…** is our supporting test for those two parts of our mission.

The third part of our mission is to *Make Disciples* and is straight out of the Great Commission, Matthew 28:19-20 (NIV) *Therefore go and make disciples of all nations, baptizing them in the name of the Father and of the Son and of the Holy Spirit, and teaching them to obey everything I have commanded you. And surely I am with you always, to the very end of the age.* If we are going to make disciples, we need first to be disciples ourselves.

Then we need to start learning how to give away what we have: our knowledge, our guidance, our service, our mission, and our finances. We then ask everyone to lead someone else into the Kingdom. So, everyone who comes to CrossPoint Church is asked to do three things: Grow, Give and Lead. That is it. Three things; worship, plug in to a small group of some kind, and give back in some way. That is our mission and our discipleship process. We try to keep is simple and easy. I've seen mission and vison statements that are so long and cumbersome that no one can repeat it and the church has a hard time living it out and keeping accountable.

We spent some time thinking about who we have been over the past 90+ years as a church. These three things kept coming to the surface...lovers of God, people who love other people, and a strong, unquenchable desire to see people grow in their faith walk with the One and Only living God. Those three things drive our mission because it's who CrossPoint Church is.

The Importance of Vision

Our vision is very different from our mission. Our vision is where we will be in five years if we live out our mission like we're supposed to, with a plan and a purpose. Our vision is where God wants us to be in five years if we are faithful to our mission and living it with intentionality. Vision changes with time and in different seasons. Vision changes as accomplishments happen and goals are met. You should NOT have the same vision today as you had five years ago. As a matter of fact, you should have reached that vision and started on a new one that God has shown you. Vision asks where will we be if we go to the mat for our mission in new ways? What can we do, what could we be, who can we reach, what will discipleship look like if we live this out full tilt, one hundred and ten percent for the next five years? This takes some time to figure out. It's not like your mission, there are few things you must do to get to vision that you did not have to do with mission.

Mission will most likely be pretty obvious for most churches…it's the reason you exist. Vision, on the other hand, must be God-driven and requires these things: prayer and fasting, knowledge of scripture to see how and what God has done in the past biblically and within the life of the congregation, and an intense study of God's movement in other churches, other leaders and in the culture.

Let me flesh out those aspects a bit because they are very important. There were many times when we stopped everything and every part of the process to pray. We would go home with a next meeting date on our calendars with the sole task of spending time in prayer for God's guidance and direction. Vision relies on God's direction alone. If it is not God's vision for you and the church do you really want to be a part of it? If it is God's vision, then you really will not have a choice. You cannot rush this process, it takes time and patience. By nature, I would have loved to rush this part of the process. Every time we hit a place in our planning sessions when we all knew we needed some prayer time there was a groan that would go out from all of us. We knew that God was in the process and that God's timing was the order of the day, not our timing. That did not make it any easier to watch deadlines drawing closer without answers.

> There came times when we all felt the pressing in of the Spirit of God. We could feel the seriousness of what was before us and knew that we were at another turning point where we might either get stonewalled or experience a huge breakthrough. At those times, we called for prayer and fasting.

There came times when we all felt the pressing in of the Spirit of God. We could feel the seriousness of what was before us and knew that we were at another turning point where we might either get stonewalled or experience a huge breakthrough. At those times, we called for prayer and fasting. I had made a commitment personally to fast from Tuesday evening to Wednesday evening each week. I did this, with only a few breaks, for over five years. On occasion, when we felt the seriousness of the issue, we would all fast and at times we called the entire congregation to fasting and prayer as well. We held teaching on fasting and offered written information on prayer and fasting. We taught our prayer teams the importance of fasting and the steps to spiritual warfare.

Everyone was challenged to go deeper in their understanding of the Bible. Each team member took the challenge through their personal devotions or as a part of a small group study. We brought our Bibles to core team staff meetings and we used them and we still do. It has given us the ability to speak God's Word to a situation or a decision and have that Word rule the day and direct us through to the end.

Along with studying the Bible we also did a study of the history of our church to discover where we have been as we looked at where we were going. In our search, we discovered that the first campus, Colonial Park, was started as a church plant in 1924. There was a

> **When we talked about our future we also talked about our past.**

vision of reaching people in new areas of Harrisburg where there where very few churches. This was a significant part of our conversations with the congregation. When we talked about our future we also talked about our past. Who we were as a church plant meant that there was a core DNA within our congregation that had been lying dormant until 2006. That's over 80 years and it was time to awaken the sleeping part of our congregation and remind them that church planting is who we are because it was how we started. How cool is that! There may be a story that your congregation that connect with that will help you lead through the change God is calling you to navigate.

Lastly, every core team staff member was challenged to go out and see what other churches looked like who were experiencing God's blessings and successes. There were times when we had to cover someone's responsibilities on a Sunday morning but it was worth it to hear what God was doing in other places. As a team of leaders, we made appointments with other church staffs so that we could pick their brains a bit. Those were some really, exciting times and we have made some lasting friendship in those places. We focused primarily on churches that were currently where we were moving towards and who had staffing structures like ours. We wanted to learn from what God was doing in other places and it was very helpful. Do not try to be a Lone Ranger leader of a staff. Change cannot be accomplished alone. If you are looking at any kind of change you are going to need to talk with other churches and leaders who have been there ahead of you. We did not travel very far but, we did travel outside of our denomination. The United Methodist Church in central Pennsylvania does not have one single church that sees one thousand in weekly average worship attendance. We believe God has called us to be a multi-site church that sees an average of one thousand in worship. That meant we needed to talk with churches who are at that level. There are plenty of churches that have made changes and who have stories to tell that can help your church make the changes God is calling you to make.

A New Name

One of the changes we found ourselves needing to make was the multisite congregations name. When we discovered the corridor of farm land that had been sold off and where all new housing was being developed, we knew that was where God was calling us. There were too many indicators and God-incidents that pointed to that area of the greater Harrisburg region. That meant that the name of the church that had been in existence since 1924 would need to change. There was a pit in the stomachs of all the leaders and staff when we would talk about the need to change the 90-year-old name. The problem was clear but the solution was not. The problem was that the name of the church was Colonial Park United Methodist Church. Colonial Park is the name of a suburb in the greater Harrisburg area. When we talked about multi-site it would inevitability come up that we could not call one location by the same name as another location in the same region. It just did not make sense for us. Those thoughts began at the end of 2004. God did not give us the new name until 2006, two years later.

We would spend time thinking and discussing the new name and would hit a stone wall, stop and allow God to talk some more. There were obviously things that were not in place yet and God needed to hold back on the whole name thing. Until one day when we were sitting together brainstorming on a new name. We wrote 20 or 30 options on a large day erase board. Then we sat back and looked at all of it. It felt like once again we were not going to get any where. Instead, we began to ask questions about the future name of the church. Questions like, why a new name, how does the name fit with the mission, how does Jesus come shining through the new name and so on? Eventually someone asked what seemed like a very simple question, "so, what is the point?" We heard the question and repeated it. "The point is God" one person said, "the point is Jesus" said someone else, "the point is the cross" and there it was! The point is the cross…CrossPoint Church. We would then be able to launch as many sites as God led us to with the overarching name of CrossPoint Church. It would look like CrossPoint @ Colonial Park, CrossPoint @ South Hanover and wherever God leads us.

We had hinted to the congregation that going multi-site would mean that we would need a new name for the church and affirmed that the entire congregation would be able to vote on the change. We could not continue to have a geographically focused name and have a presence in other communities. When everything came together to make the name CrossPoint happen we began thinking about how we were going to present the change. First, we were going to tie it intricately to the new vision we would be launching in January, 2007.

The new vision included dynamic new things and we were convinced that the church would never be the same, so, how could the old name describe a church with a radical focus on the cross?

Second, CrossPoint Church was very similar to the previous name of Colonial Park Church and we stressed the similarities. The initials of CrossPoint Church are the same as Colonial Park Church: CPC. For many years, people had been referring to Colonial Park Church as CPC. We had been using the initials in many places and people had been doing things like making checks out to CPC so moving to CrossPoint Church did not change the CPC and people were thrilled, especially when we showed them that it would be CrossPoint @ Colonial Park. It was a plus that we used as often as we could to help the congregation make the move.

Third, the church had made the move from Colonial Park United Methodist Church to Colonial Park Church (A United Methodist Congregation) in the late 1990's with the change in vision. So, the fact that the denomination was not a part of the name was not an issue.

Fourth, we had something incredible going for us that we did not realize was going to be as instrumental to the success of changing the name of a 90+ year old church as it was. We stressed the importance of needing a new name so that those persons at the other campuses would see themselves as valid members of something larger than any one campus. We taught the importance of sacrificing a little for Kingdom gain. The name of the church now offered a focus and it spoke volumes about what we are about…the whole point is the cross; it is who we are and what we teach. Now, our new name would reflect that truth.

But, there is a whole lot more to coming up with a new name than brainstorming or presentation. We called in an expert in the field of graphics who helped us create a logo that we could brand. We had done enough reading about branding to know its importance in making change stick for the people who knew us for what we used to be. Not only did we need to change an entire congregation's use of the old name to the new name, we had to change an entire community's knowledge of who we were. We needed to let the greater Harrisburg area know that the church they had known for many years as Colonial Park Church was now CrossPoint Church. We brought in several consultants who listened to what we wanted to accomplish with the logo. They in turn spent a week putting together drafts of what a new logo could look like. As a team we listened to their presentations and chose the company we liked best.

We ended up going with a small, local firm. We knew the owner because at one point he was a worship leader at one of our weekend services. More importantly, he knew us. He knew our names, he knew the churches DNA, he knew my heart and how I felt about Jesus and the Church. As a leader those things were invaluable to me and to the process. His name is Karl and he taught us the importance of color choices and how certain colors elicit certain feelings. He taught us about fonts and pitches and so much more. In the end, after several drafts and tweakings, we finally arrived at our logo. Karl would send us a few options and we would all gather around and say what we liked and did not like. Once we had our thoughts together we'd send them back to Karl. He would implement them and send them back to us for review. There were times when we had to trust Karl's expertise and we asked him for his educated opinion. We all poured our heart into that logo and now we had something to present to the congregation and the community.

Don't miss this: we put the new logo into the vision plan so that when we talked about the new five-year vision the logo was never far from the conversation. They went together, a package deal, all or nothing. I cannot stress the importance of making change in this way if you want to experience success. We needed it to be obvious to everyone that we were not making change for change sake, but were making a significant turn in how we were going to be seen from now on and what things we were going to hold on to as the vital and important as a congregation. The new name and logo stated to the community a new strength and presence that would make a difference and, more importantly, was grounded in the cross of Christ.

Yes, I can hear your question – "does everyone like the new name?" The answer is no. There are people who have been at our first campus for hundreds of years (okay, a bit of an exaggeration). Some of them still say things like, "it will always be Colonial Park Church to me." In some ways, we tell them that they are right. If you go to the Colonial Park campus it will always be CrossPoint @ Colonial Park. So, we are able to support their thoughts that it will always be Colonial Park because they're right. The name of the community is not going to change which is the identifier for all our campuses. CrossPoint @ Colonial Park, CrossPoint @ South Hanover, and CrossPoint @ Rutherford, and soon, CrossPoint @ Mid-Town, are all community locations. The CrossPoint name and logo provides connection and offers an umbrella over all campuses uniting them together under one mission and vision as one church at each location.

Now, let me say this about name; the name does not make the church. That might sound like a no brainer, but the temptation will be great to think that changing the name of the church will set up a long list of other changes that you might be hoping for. Name change does not bring change to a congregation. A congregation moves toward a new direction that forces a name change, not the other way around.

If you are thinking that it would be great to have one of those cool church names, take a look at the top 100 churches in America today. Willow Creek, Fellowship, The Village, North Point and Saddleback are not names that are all that thrilling. They are geographic locations or rather churchy sounding. In a world that seems to be telling churches to be more post modern and culturally relevant these churches are doing some of the best work in the nation and yet do not have really, catchy, cool names. It's not a name change that will turn things around but, it is a must if you're going to move everyone forward under a new vision.

Reflection Questions:

+ How do you feel about your current level of preparedness for change as a leader and as a congregation? What do you need to do to be better prepared?

+ What can you do to make your mission statement simple and easy for everyone to remember?

+ What vision of the future is starting to take shape? How will you start to develop/discover a vision for the future?

+ Who are you talking with inside and outside the church about the changes you feel God is calling you to make?

+ Have you scheduled times for prayer and fasting and listening?

+ Does the current name of your church reflect the mission and/ or vision of the church?

Chapter 3
What the Vision Requires of a Leader

One of the books that was critical to our process was *Breakout Churches* by Thom Rainer. Our whole team and our church council read the book together at the recommendation of Steve Clay, our mission/vision consultant. The book highlights churches who plateaued, hit a crisis moment, and then broke out to become great churches. It contains the principles laid out in *Good to Great* by Jim Collins (our staff also read this together) that so many of us are familiar with today. Rainer identifies the key to breaking out is strong, solid leadership that is willing to take the time, energy and effort needed to walk a congregation through the deep valley and out the other side. In my experience, most pastors, staff, and congregational leaders do not want to work that hard.

Change is hard work and there are a lot of people who go into "church work" or volunteer for a board because they thought it would be easy. The epiphany that happened when our new name became obvious to our staff came only after two years, multiple brainstorming sessions and a whole slew of names going up in flames on a dry erase board. There were long nights when the staff had dinner together after having lunch together and did not get home in time to tuck the kids into bed. There were long retreats, meetings at our homes and lots of phone and email conversations. Impromptu meetings would be called around the central hub of the business office at any given time. Bill Hybels characterizes this as the willingness to sleep on the cot, to get the job done no matter what it takes. John Maxwell calls it *the Law of Sacrifice* (from *21 Irrefutable Laws of Leadership*).

That is the kind of staff (paid and unpaid) we became through the process. I do not think we started out being that kind of staff. We went into this thinking that this would be easy since we were the staff of a church that always seemed primed for the next adventure. And I watched as truths from *Good to Great* lived themselves out right in front of me. For example, we had one loved staff member who decided to step off the staff or what is affectionately called voting herself off the bus. It was just too much, considering her family situation, and we supported her decision completely. Her role on staff and her passion for special needs ministries drove us to place special needs awareness and accessibility to all ministries as a key component of the five-year vision we launched in 2007. Her work was complete and it was time to exit. We had to trust that God would provide and He has.

We also watched other leaders transition from who they used to be and the role they lived out every day to something almost completely different to fit the new vision. The choir director became the Director of Music and Worship. It was not the position she was hired for. That was a different bus at a different time. She made the jump to the new bus and she never wanted to go back because the new mission and vision are energizing - notice, not easy, just energizing. It is incredibly exciting and exhilarating but, it is also very draining. It is the kind of stuff that will get you out of bed in the morning or quite possibly wake you up in the middle of the night with a solution to a transition that needs to happen or maybe to pray some more. Don't do all of this just because you think you want to change the name of the church or you want change for the sake of change because the church is dead or dying. Do it because you have no choice. God has called you to it and you cannot surrender to anything less than full submission.

I want you to hear me clearly: this vision thing is a leadership thing. I was not a great leader when I had the position dropped into my lap. I'm still not a great leader. I have my moments and I still have people pointing things out to me that I need to be doing (or not doing). I want to be a great leader. I believe that is what we're called to be in the *Great* Commandment and the *Great* Commission. As Thom Rainer points out, it's a sin to be good when we are called to be great. In the past two years, I have read no less than twenty-two different books ranging from *Creative Leadership* and *Making Leadership Stick* to *Blue Like Jazz* and *The Barbarian Way*. I went back and reread Brother Laurence's *The Practice of the Presence of God*. I recommitted myself to God's word. I have read a minimum of one chapter of the Bible a day.

Three years ago I made the decision to read and reread the book of Acts through out the entire year. I read through Acts 11 times in 2007. Two years ago, I read through 1 and 2 Corinthians and last year it was Romans. This year I am reading through the entire Bible using the Chronological One Year Bible. My recommitment to the Word has brought the biggest blessing to me. I believe I speak better and live better because of my time in the Word. Let me say this as a must for your vision and a ground zero for your life, get into the Word deeply, daily, passionately if you're going to be a part of a congregational change in the Kingdom of God.

Another thing I began to do with success was journaling. I began to realize several years ago that I was going through a major transitional time in my life and leadership. One of the best ways I know to unload feelings and thoughts about what God is doing is through the spiritual discipline of journaling. I have never journaled with success before and I was hopeful that this time it would stick. The pressure of all the changes has forced out of me some serious journaling and it has stuck with an intensity that I did not anticipate. It is good to be able to go back and look at what I thought, what we have done together as a church, and what was going through my head. The spiritual disciplines have been incredibly helpful. Do not underestimate the enemy or your need for preparation, renewal and refueling through a deep spiritual connection with the Father. Waves that crash into people who are weak or unprepared reek untold levels of damage that can undo any work invested up to that point.

I am a firm believer in the spiritual disciplines as a preventative to spiritual weakness and I believe that as leaders we need to be as grounded as humanly possible so that God has as much spirituality to work with as you can possibly offer. There are going to be times when as a leader, you are going to be required to go deep into the well-spring of your life to offer hope, direction or healing. If you are not spending time making sure that the well is being replenished, you will come up empty at best. At worst, you'll come up with muck and trash that is worthless or even harmful to those you've been called to minister within the Kingdom of an almighty and splendid King.

If you are going to give your life to something meaningful like congregational change, you need to make sure you are doing it for the right reasons. Just hoping that it is all going to be okay or that the forward movement of the mission and vision is not dependent on you is an equally profound lie. God wants to use people just like you to do something amazing in the world so that the glory of God can be seen. Too many church leaders are trying to wing it when God requires us to be faithful and obedient. The mission and vision of your church has the God-desired potential to change lives in your neighborhood and around the globe. It requires all you have and all you can give.

> If you are going to give your life to something meaningful like congregational change, then you need to make sure you're doing it for the right reasons.

Now, do not get me wrong. I am not suggesting that you live your life in such a way that you focus only on the mission/vision of the church you are at. It is not God's desire for any of us to gain what seems like the entire world only to lose that which is the most precious. Each leader, each staff member, each pastor needs to spend time setting boundaries and needs to know where the line in the sand gets drawn. For me, my family is important and valuable to me and is the first place where I am called to minister and give my life away. If I am giving everything I have to the Church, to the mission and vision, and have nothing left for the people God has given to me to love and cherish as family, I believe I am grieving the very heart of God by my misguided living. If I can keep a proper balance of life and family and work and vocation and relationships, I believe God smiles with joy over me in those moments.

That does not mean that there are not times of sacrifice that effects everyone around you. When we moved into the season of catastrophic change I sat down with my family, you know...one of those family meetings, and we talked candidly about what the next few months and years were going to look like. There would be changes but, I was still going to be there and be available. I let them know that there were going to be some long days and late nights. I asked everyone to be a part of what God wanted to do. I promised that this would be a "season", not a new way of understanding our family or a "new normal." Each member of my family and many of the family members of the staff took the challenge and made many sacrifices to see what God wanted to accomplish in us and in His church. There are church members and entire families who have gone far above and beyond what was is normally expected to see God's vision for us become a reality. What a blessing to be a part of such a movement of God.

Reflection Questions:

+ How will you and the people who are leading your church into a time of change spend time reading, studying, meditating on the Bible?
+ What other books are you reading to prepare yourself for the work of change and transformation?
+ What spiritual disciplines do you currently practice or do you need to implement that will be helpful to you as you manage and navigate the change God has for the church?
+ What are the staffing areas you will need to address? Why?

Chapter 4
One Church - Three Campuses

So, as you can see, there were several catastrophic things that happened to this mainline church that became the catalyst for transformational change. The first was the unsettledness of the leadership in a time of plateau. When leaders get unsettled God can open windows and door. The second was the refinement of our mission statement and a new vision based on that mission. The loss of the lead pastor was the third catastrophic event in the life of the church. The development of a new leadership model was the fourth. The fifth was the congregations' name change. The sixth was launching two new campuses at the same time. Any one of these things has the potential to bring a wave of change crashing into the congregational life of a church. Let's talk about that sixth one for a moment.

After making the decision to launch a multi-site church, we began considering the ways to accomplish this new and bold vision God had dropped on us. When we discovered multi-site, and realized through the one-day workshop with Community Christian Church of Naperville, IL that it was the direction we needed to go, we moved forward with the plan. We identified who would be the leader of the new campus and how we would manage that leadership between campuses. We rearranged our staff picture so that we could hire a new youth pastor and free me up to become the teaching pastor. We made the decision that the teaching pastor would travel back and forth on Sunday mornings between the two campuses whose services would be at times that allowed for the necessary travel time (20 minutes). We hired a new, part-time youth pastor in July of 2005 and moved him to full-time within six months so that I could dedicate all my time in 2006 to starting the new site in 2007. While searching for a location for the new faith community we entered conversations with an existing United Methodist Church that was struggling and did not have a positive future.

From two to three...

In 2006 we started having conversations with a team of leaders and the pastor from a neighboring United Methodist Church that was staring at an uncertain future. This team of leaders was tasked with looking at possibilities for the survival of this congregation and they were looking at every option. So, when they heard about CrossPoint launching a new campus they began to ask if they could be one of our campuses as well. We were not opposed so we joined the conversation. We knew that the way had already been blazed by Community Christian Church in the Chicago area. They had absorbed an existing congregation and property about a year before us so we knew we had someone who could tell us how to do it. That is a principle that we have lived out all along the path of change. The principle is: if someone else has done it before us, call them, visit them, talk to them, because there's no reason for us to repeat the failures and to face the same stumbling blocks that they had. If someone has done it already then, we need to learn from them. That might be the reason you are reading this book, because you're looking to see how someone else did what you believe God is challenging you and/or your church to begin.

Our conversations with our third location began a full year and a half before the union took place. The first thing we learned is that this kind of transition takes time, a long time. People need to process this kind of information and ask questions along the way. The other thing I learned is the that the staff and volunteers who were committed were moving faster than the rest of the congregation. Those who were vested were ready to make the move but, most people who are connected to a church as members or attenders move at a different pace than the people who work and serve at the church. Sometimes it is a good thing to slow down and make sure that everyone is on board. Notice I did not say everyone agrees, just that they understand what the change will entail.

Principle of Movement

There is a principle that is important to consider for a moment. Those who attend church and most of the members will think about their church once or twice a week. For many, their thoughts about church happen Saturday evening when they consider if they're going tomorrow and if so, what they might wear. They don't spend a great deal of time thinking about the series you are preaching on or what song they hope to sing. They're not thinking about praying about what the pastor might want to teach them or show them when they show up tomorrow. For the most part they are caught up in the busyness of living life: kids, job or career, making ends meet, retirement planning, do I have enough life insurance, or is the weather going to be nice for the barbeque this weekend. Their world does not revolve around the church like it does for the paid staff and unpaid volunteers who are investing a lot of time and energy each week to make worship, children and youth ministries, missions, and small groups all happen with as few glitches as possible.

For the majority of people, church is something they think about on the way to the worship facility on Sunday morning. They are a great group of people who are loyal and growing in their walk with God. They love their church and would not go anywhere else but, they are out of the loop when it comes to what God is doing at the heart of their church. They get their news about church on Sunday morning even though things are happening every day. This group is made up of people who come to church because it's the right thing to do. They bring their children and help out when they can. When their friends talk about looking for a church they recommend theirs.

Then there are those members and attenders who are excited about their church. They were at the church at least once during the week, they checked the web site or read the pastors blog at least once or twice during the time in between Sunday mornings. They were together with a class or a small group of some kind on Sunday morning or during the week. Their faith and trust in God is solid. They are the people who are wondering what God is doing next because they want to be a part of God's move in their church and community. These are the movers in their congregation who will take their church to the next place that God is preparing the soil for growth and outreach. They don't tend to sit too long before they start asking about what's next.

A few years ago, I learned an important axiom from Ron Silvia, pastor at The Springs in Ocala, FL. Ron mentioned that he loves everyone at The Springs but, he moves with those who are moving. What he is saying is, as a pastor or church leader it is our biblical responsibility to love all of those that God brings into our ministry arena. But, when it comes to what we put our energies or efforts into, what we're willing go the extra mile for, we pick those people who are moving out in front, those persons who are asking the "what's next" question.

When we launched our second site, it was that group of excited and committed church members who made up the launch team. There were over 30 people who were ready for what God wanted to do next in their lives and in the life of the CrossPoint Church. Their excitement and commitment to the Kingdom is what saw them through the difficult times that happened during the launch and throughout the years of establishing the site and reaching critical mass. While I will be present for everyone in the congregation as their pastor, I tend to devote and commit time and energy to those who are moving the mission and vision of the church forward. Not everyone is going to move the church forward. As a pastor/leader you are called to love everyone who shows up to your church. It is important to know how to balance your time so that you are committing the larger part of your ministry energies into those people who are taking God's mission and vision seriously enough to go all out with you. An important principle to remember along the way is that leaders invest in other leaders.

Here is an important principle we learned…those who are the weekly attenders will take longer to process a move of God and the things that God wants to accomplish in their church. They deal with the information once a week. They tend not to take home the plans God is giving to the church and really pray over them or spend time discussing them with other members/attenders. They think about the church each week when they arrive and they will process what they heard over lunch that day but, when the stuff of life invades, the plans God has for your church get lost in the rush. We learned that the time we get with people on Sunday morning was invaluable. We discovered that we needed to use some of our Sunday morning space and time to present what God was challenging us to do in our region (greater Harrisburg, PA). With most of the members of your church, Sunday morning is the only time a leader gets so, you have to use things like posters, ministry centers, photographs, progress thermometers, refrigerator magnets, and anything else the marketers tell you work well in your area. Weekly worshippers need as many formats as you can use to help them to see, hear, and come in contact with what God is telling their church to accomplish.

> "Those who are the weekly attenders will take longer to process a move of God and the things that God wants to accomplish in your church."

The Principle of Momentum

There is another significant principle that we discovered…too late. It is the principle of momentum. This principle says that there is always a level of momentum in yourself and in the congregation. It is vital to understand what that level of momentum is before you start to do a major change. New things should always be done out of a place of positive momentum. That means that you, personally, or the congregation collectively have experienced a number of positive events that have gotten you or everyone excited about what is possible and what the future could be like. A few "wins" early in the process can make a huge difference in the momentum of the congregation. Conversely, a series of difficult experiences can cause a feeling of negative momentum that will work to convince you or the congregation that the future is bleak and this is not a good time for change.

It is important to take the pulse of the leadership as well as the congregation. Leaders can get excited about the future and the potential changes because they are living with them every day. The congregation may be in a completely different place. When we started our second campus we did so out of a place of predominately negative momentum. A majority of the congregation had not yet processed the loss of the previous senior pastor nor, were they ready to head into change with me, the new guy.

Even though I had been there for 10 years I was now in a new position and people needed time to get used to that change before we started changing all the other stuff. I would go back and do that differently if I could. I would have pulled back the reins and waited until we pulled out of the negative momentum and into the positive. It is possible to move a congregation from a place of negative momentum into a place of positive momentum. It is also possible to do things that will take a congregation from positive to negative as well.

Instead of dealing with the things that were causing negative momentum, I chose to work with a group who were excited about the future and launching a new campus and who were excited about the possibilities of reaching a new area for Jesus. It was positive momentum but, it was not shared throughout the entire congregation. Admittedly, I did not want to wait…I had a team of wild horses and I wanted to set them loose. I have apologized for that since then. Make sure that when you go into change, that you have taken the time to get people excited and help them see the positives, in an effort to build momentum among the congregants.

Establish the Problem

I said that there are things you can do to move a congregation from negative to positive momentum. God's plan for change needs to be a part of what you preach about and how you plan your events. Your Sunday morning messages should include some part of the change God is calling you to lead this congregation through. Understanding the reason for the change is the first thing that needs established. Andy Stanley talks about the establishment of the problem in his series on leadership. A key element in counting the cost of the project is first stating why things need to change. A fair number of people will tell you that things are fine, change is not needed because they are happy, therefore everything is going good, don't rock the boat. Without a clearly communicated problem they are right. There is no reason to go through the pain and hardship of catastrophic change if there is not a clear rationale. For you and your church there needs to be a clear reason why you exist. If you are not clear on what the reason is, then that is your first hurdle. Call together a group of people who are at varying degrees of commitment to your church (including some who are not committed at all) and ask them why they think your church exists. What problem(s) are we here to solve? If your church were to disappear tomorrow would anyone miss its presence?

> "Call together a group of people who are at varying degrees of commitment to you church and ask them why they think your church exists. What problem(s) are we here to solve? If your church were to disappear tomorrow would anyone miss its presence?"

The problem should then be woven into everything you do and say. Solving the problem becomes a central part of the yard stick you use to evaluate whether you should be doing a ministry, an event, a sermon series, small groups, soup kitchens, clothing banks and the whole long list of things churches do. That means the problem needs to be central to the gospel so that no matter what you are doing the problem can be directed by God's Word.

Outreach and internal events can all be useful tools in helping people move from just doing church to being a church with a plan and a purpose. I cannot express enough the importance of this step. You are unique as a congregation. You have a unique DNA, a distinctive location, a one of a kind personality. That means you are positioned to reach people with that mix of characteristics. Don't over look the significance of the genuineness of who you are as a congregation and God's ability to draw people to you through that wonderful blending. You are positioned to offer to your community that distinctive role which God has given to you alone. Your congregation is unlike any other so that you can reach those people who other congregations can not reach.

Our problem at Colonial Park Church was that the statistics were showing that there was a large number of people in the area who are unchurched. Each Sunday there were people who did not see going to church as a viable option. We looked up the statistics and discovered that there were approximately 125,000 people who did not attend a church on any given weekend. That was a problem. So, we believed that launching another church would help people find their way to God. We also knew that there were spiritual problems in the Harrisburg area that were affecting the souls of the people and the heart of the region. That was a problem. So, we started talking about "making it hard to go to hell from Harrisburg" as a slogan or catch phrase. It was edgy and crazy but, it was easy to say, easy to remember, and easy to understand. Problems get people mad, excited, focused, and determined. It's important to establish what problems your church is here in the world to solve.

Launching One, Transitioning Another

The plan to launch a new campus came together and the opportunity to transition an existing congregation presented itself to us at the same time. That meant we were working on two different fronts. To be honest, we were working on three fronts but, we had forgotten about the first site a bit while we were focusing on launching/transitioning the two new sites. Here are the steps we took to move into launching our second site. Earlier I mentioned that we had gone to a workshop that was hosted by Community Christian Church from the greater Chicago area. That was the starting place for our planning our first launch. We walked though the step by step evaluation process that they had established. We discovered that all we needed to complete the process was a location. We spent a great deal of time searching for a suitable location and after almost a year we found the local elementary school to be the perfect spot. During the time when we were searching we were also doing several other things as well. We were preparing the congregation, evaluating finances and recruiting the leaders who were going to be the launch team.

Our preparations of the congregation included several things that we see now, in retrospect, were key elements. The first was our participation in the Purpose Driven material out of Saddleback Church in California as a spiritual preparation for the future God had in store for us. The church was a part of the pilot project when Saddleback decided to launch the Purpose Driven Church on a national level. We also piloted "The Purpose Driven Life" and "The 40 Days of Purpose" projects. We used those teachings to present the foundational truths about who we are and what the purpose of the Church is truly all about. The Purpose Driven teaching caused a general stirring among the people to not only discover who we are but, to begin to live beyond what the church was currently doing in the areas of worship, missions, and outreach. This unsettledness among church members led the way for the leaders to present plans for new changes that would make the possibilities a reality.

It is important to stop for a moment and make something painfully clear. This move took years to take root. We engaged in specific teaching for years to prepare the way for the changes God wanted to bring to CrossPoint Church. I cannot emphasize this enough; this kind of catastrophic change takes a great deal of ground work to prepare the hearts of the people who make up your congregation.

We went through years of purposeful teaching that opened people's hearts and spiritual eyes to the things God wanted to accomplish in and through us. We developed a system of spiritual discipleship that equipped people for what God desired. Our whole membership process was redesigned to include a spiritual gifts assessment as well as a personal discipleship piece that challenges every person who wants to be a member to get involved in an identified ministry or mission. We fundamentally changed what it means to be a church member of CrossPoint.

Those things had to happen first before we could challenge people toward major changes. Most mainline churches have been functioning out of a mentality that all we have to do is open our doors, go through the proposed liturgy, offer the sacraments and people will show up. We cannot just open the doors and expect people to show up. There was a day when that was true but, that is not how our society works today. Mainline churches must experience major, possibly even catastrophic changes that will move them forward into the 21st century.

With the growing gap between the church and culture in mind that is the mark of the 21st century our church moved into a time of focusing in on the importance of mission, vision, and outreach as the central focus of why we existed as a church in this time, for this generation. We set up everything in the context of our mission and vision to touch a region for Jesus Christ and His Kingdom. Our weekly Sunday morning messages included elements of the mission and vision so that people would begin to understand the connection between what we were doing and God's design, as found in scripture. It is essential to show that what God has given you to do has been supported in God's Word in every way.

If you are going to survive catastrophic change you have to make certain, in everyone's mind, that it is not your idea or your plan but, God's divine guidance. Anything less will not only fail, anything less than God's move will cause you headaches and heartaches that will keep you up at night and frustrate you to a place of ineffectiveness and possibly even surrender. Be certain to communicate clearly that the changes you are suggesting are because God has a directive or command that as a leader and a congregation you must follow. To do anything less is to be disobedient.

People in a church that is changing to reach a generation or meet a recognized regional need based on a concise, biblical mandate will find it hard to argue with the changes. That does not mean that people will not leave. Will you will need to constantly remind people of the cause, the mission and the vision. In the words of Andy Stanley: "vision leaks." You have to constantly interpret, proclaim, remind and reiterate the mission and vision of the church you are leading. Remember, the majority of people who attend a church that is changing only think about it once a week – Sunday morning. You think about it all the time, it keeps you up at night and can consume your everyday life in ministry. So, when members do not get it or seem to lose track of the reason that things are not the way they used to be, it is not their fault. It is the task of the leaders to constantly remind them of why the change is needed. The task of leaders is to communicate that reason (or problem) clearly and often, sometimes to the point of exhaustion. Those who are there each week should hear something about the vision and mission each week.

Now, doing all the things that others tell you to do and following the God-given plan doesn't mean it will be easy. One of the most troubling aspects of this process is the "human factor." There will be some who just cannot get their brains around what God is doing and will, in turn, blame the pastor and the leaders for hijacking their church. One of the books I read that helped me understand this dynamic was a booked called: "Who Stole My Church?" by Gordon MacDonald. I highly recommend it. For some people, the change that is happening is too much. They may have been members who had lost the fire and this new move toward a God-given vision does not line up with who they are now or where they're at today. And they will leave because the direction of the church does not match up with what God has put into their hearts to accomplish. Let me say this, there is absolutely nothing wrong with someone leaving your fellowship because they believe God is calling them to fulfill the Great Commandment or Great Commission in some other way or in some other place.

As a matter of fact, if they are feeling that way and they don't leave, they will cause problems down the road. Actually, it might be best for some people to leave. For those who were just hanging on, this new move of the church can either excite them back into the fellowship or push them out the door. It will hurt when people leave, especially when they just don't like what is happening or what you are doing. Change generates deep feelings in people and for some, it brings out the worst. The best leaders develop ways to help people leave as best as they can for both parties and for the Kingdom. That includes attenders and members as well as paid and unpaid leaders.

And let me add this, some of the people who leave will surprise you. They were the ones you thought would be the movers and shakers of this new, God-given change. They may have been close to you, or even a part of the brainstorming process or design team. There is something about what's going on that they just cannot go along with. It may be God-driven, it may be something else and if you are fortunate, they will come to you one day and tell you that it is time for them to go…they have found another church. And you did not even know they were looking, right? They stayed long enough to hear the vision and the plan being fleshed out and developed and they made the decision that this was not for them.

As a church and as a leader - be gracious. I know it hurts. With every person who walks out the door and never comes back you begin questioning the plan. You might find yourself asking God, "did I do something wrong, did I hear you right…why are they leaving if this is of you, God?" Hear me when I say this: not everyone will stay, not everyone can make it through the change, not everyone is called to what God is calling your church to do. It is okay. It is okay to cry when they leave. It is okay to pray for them when they leave. It is okay to hug them in the grocery store when you have that awkward encounter. And it is okay when it feels like they took a part of your heart, a part of your family with them. That is what it means to be a church, a member of a congregation, a pastor…sometimes people leave us and it hurts. In the almost 30 years I have been in ministry I have never gotten used to people leaving.

Now, that is not to say that there are not persons who should leave. There are the disgruntled, divisive, gossiping, spiritually anemic people who will constantly cause a ruckus during the changes. On occasion, you may need to show one or two people where the door is. I can remember several people who came to me (and sometimes at me) with such frequency that I finally had to ask them why they were still at CrossPoint. The one guy said he was no longer sure and that he thought that it was a sign that he should leave. I agreed with him and he is happy now at another church, as far as I know. This gets difficult when there are people whom everyone loves but, who need to go.

Staffing for movement toward fulfilling mission and vision

When it becomes clear that catastrophic change is imminent, it is important to start asking questions about how you are staffed for the changes that God is bringing your way. As a leader, you need to analyze the gifts and talents that God has blessed you with when it comes to your staff. The staff is vitally important to the success of what God wants to do at your church. These are the people who will work at the ground level and who will make the vision a reality. Some of the staff are people who got you to the edge of the changes you are facing but, may not be the same people who will take you through the change. This truth is as important for the small church as it is for the medium and large church. The small church is often staffed by volunteers who can be just as powerful, influential, and entrenched as the paid staff of a medium or large church. I have done consultations at small churches where part of the recommendation for change was to remove a volunteer who was influencing every decision away from the needed changes that God was encouraging the congregation to adopt.

Also, be willing to think outside the box. One of our best staff members through the entire change was Barb, our office manager. The position of office manager is the hub of your organization. Every piece of information comes into the hub and then back out to the right department or team. It's crucial that the person who is the hub of your church is on board with the mission and vision, if not it can be devastating. Barb is not a member of our church, she attends another local UM congregation nearby. But, Barb has the mission and vision of our church tattooed on her heart. She eats and breaths CrossPoint Church. She is a "sleep on the cot," give 110% kind of person and we would not be where we are today without her. Thank you, Barb!

The person(s) who answers the phone, the volunteers who help fold the weekly programs, the custodial staff, the ushers and greeters are all equally important in moving the church into significant and life altering change. No less or no more important are the paid and unpaid persons who are the youth leaders, children's ministry directors, education directors, worship and arts directors, secretaries, facilities managers, worship leaders and all the other staff possibilities.

There are those leaders who are not skilled to take the church to it is next level. They were instrumental in getting the church to the edge of change and their gifts were vital in getting you there. But, there is a principle at work, those who got you here may not get you there. Those are some of the most difficult discussions with friends and staff. They will break you heart and crush your soul. To walk through those conversations, you must keep your eye on the vision God has given to you and your church. Remember, God knows who those people are and what they need and God will provide.

First, establish what is needed from each ministry area in order to see the change through to the next level. Every ministry area, paid and unpaid, should have a job description that clearly explains the work that the person in that positon should be doing. It should be clear in the job

> The vision of a ministry area needs to have clarity and focus as is supports the greater vision and mission of the church.

description how this position contributes to the overall mission and vision of the church. No single area is sacred or can be left out of the plan. There are a great number of church staff and volunteers who have no idea what it is they are supposed to be doing other than whatever it was they did last week. The vision of a ministry area needs to have clarity and focus as it supports the greater vision and mission of the church. To do what we did last week but expect different results is a form of insanity.

Between formal training and life experience there are not a whole lot of places where people can get a new paradigm about how to set the world on fire for Jesus through his Church. Personally, I have found most of my inspiration in non-denominational settings where the training and years of "doing it this way" don't exist. There are some places that I've visited where it seems that they function totally out of a mind set that no one said we couldn't so we did and it worked. As a leader of the entire church, an area ministry leader/director, a paid staff or an unpaid volunteer; pastoral leaders need to make sure that we are communicating what it is we expect this ministry to look like.

Once the set of needs are clearly defined, the second thing to do is to challenge the current leaders to step up to the task by honing their skills or fine tuning the gifts that are required. No one wants to see a dedicated leader be let go because their leadership skills have plateaued. A clear challenge to move to the next level in leadership may be a motivator to the leader who has reached their tipping point. As an overseer, your task is to be clear about what is needed. Too many people sit in jobs where the duties are not clearly defined. An equally important part of the job of the overseer is to be willing to guide the leader in either stepping up or stepping off the bus. By offering the appropriate time needed to digest what is required, debrief what is desired with trusted people, and process the information you offer - the leaders under you will have the opportunity to ponder and pray over the choices that need made. Empowering the leaders of ministry areas in this way gives the authority to the person to decide to stay or to move on to a place where their skills and gifts might be a better fit to move the church forward.

Reflection Questions:

+ Before you move forward you should be clear on what problem God has given you and your church the vision to solve. What problem exists in your community that your congregation has been positioned to solve?

+ What tools (books, etc.) are you working through together as a staff and as a church that will open everyone up to a new paradigm?

+ What would it take to make sure that all ministries and staff (paid and unpaid) are aligned with the mission and vision?

+ Where are you and your congregation in the area of momentum? Rate yourself on a scale of 1-10, 1 being lousy and 10 being jumping out of your skin.

+ How will the church support and bless those who are not aligned to leave? How can you make it possible for people to leave with grace and love?

Chapter 5
Finances

Adjust finances toward mission and vision

Most churches set their budgets around three or four key areas like programs/ministries, staff/pastors and utilities/facilities, etc. If you and the church you are leading are going to do something as dynamic as transition an existing congregation or launch a new campus or plant a new church you will need to rework how you think about the finances you are responsible for. The budget of your church will need to be examined with a fine-tooth comb. There will need to be a willingness on your part to look at everything the church is committing finances toward.

That means you may have to put some sacred cows on display so that they can be examined for their viability and contribution to the vision. This is not to be cruel but to make an honest examination of every ministry that the church is currently doing to make sure they align with the vision. Transformation and/or church planting takes a great deal of energy and focus. Any ministry that distracts from that focus will need to do one of two things: commit to aligning the resources they are currently using toward the vision or dissolve or dismantle the ministry so that the resources they currently use can be reallocated toward the vision.

You will first need to look for those ministries that align already or, with a slight adjustment, can be tweaked to fit into a supportive or even a primary position in the new vision. Without a doubt, there will be several ministries that already fit where your church is going as you live out the vision. Those ministries that are committed to outreach, evangelism, local missions, etc. can all be combined and used to begin a line item that is solely dedicated to the vision of transitioning or planting. If the plan God has given your church is going to see success it will need to have the entire church supporting it.

This first group will be the easiest, but do not be fooled, it may take some time to accomplish this needed adjustment. There will be people who have invested their lives into these ministries and may be slow in their willingness to move or surrender the funds they have watched over, possibly for years. Meetings will need to be held where the vision of the church is shared with those leaders, staff and members, and volunteers where they can hear the plans your church has for the future. They will need time to think about it, process it and buy into the vision for what God wants to do with your church in building the Kingdom. The senior leader(s) will need to listen to those who have been doing and managing these ministries and missions in such a way that the concerns they have can be heard and addressed.

Eliminate areas of expense that do not support the mission/vision

You also need to look for ministries that are obsolete and no longer support the mission, vision, and core values of the church. Here is where life as a leader can get real tough. The investment people have in their church is sometimes wrapped up in something from the past that is no longer bringing transformation for the Kingdom. Pastor Andy Stanley of Northpoint Church in Atlanta, GA calls these the "ugly sofas." They were once in style, the height of fashion in their day but, now they are out of fashion and no one wants to sit in them. The people who bought them are convinced they are still important because there is a nostalgia attached to them. Memories were made there. Those sofas are just memory holders (as well as a few coins and a piece of gum or two) and they are no longer able to take the vision forward.

The senior leader(s) will need to hold gatherings with people who are invested in those outdated ministries or missions that no longer find themselves aligned with the direction the church is going. You cannot avoid or run from these very important times when the vision is cast and where people learn that it will affect their sacred cow mission and/or ministry. And let me warn you, these meetings can be ugly. People don't like change, especially when it means that a ministry or mission that helped them grow, changed the way they believed, or had a powerful influence in the lives of others will no longer be around. We've had to cut ministries to get us to the place where we could make significant changes. Those ministries were valuable in getting us where we were, but would hold us back from going where God wanted us to go.

An example might be a ministry where only a few people are focused on worship design. As change happens you might find you have multiple services, multiple venues for worship and multiple sites where worship takes place. The old model can no longer meet the need that the change has brought and a new model or ministry needs to develop. Earlier, I mentioned that no ministry is exempt from a full audit of its' effectiveness.

This is the time to audit every ministry area. We call these audits "autopsies" and they help us ask important questions about the viability of a position or a ministry or an event in moving us closer to the vision. If there are tangible ways that we can see the mission and vision being fulfilled and moving forward, we are willing to keep it going. If not,

> We've learned that we need to commit ministry and mission monies toward those new areas that are mission/vision focused.

we will strongly consider cutting that item and moving the funds that were allocated to that area or event over to something that has a proven track record of promoting the vision. We have learned that we need to commit ministry and mission monies toward those new areas that are mission/vision focused.

In October of each year our ministry leaders and their teams start looking at the budgets that they are going to submit for the coming year. Each ministry area team is responsible to submit their part of the budget. It then goes to the executive team who reviews the numbers and asks questions back to the ministry leader/team or to make recommendations based on what the overall budget can handle and what the Church Councils evaluation of the coming year might be. Each ministry area leader or team must be willing to defend its numbers and show how their ministry fits into the mission and will advance the vision that currently is in place. If there is an area that has not shown positive results, we have had to make the hard decision to cut that ministry or event.

Also, do not be afraid to look for funds from outside your church as well. We happen to be part of a large denomination who has a heart for launching new churches. When it came time to start seeing where the money was going to come from, we asked the denomination if they would be willing to put their money where their hearts were. And they said yes. We received a $100,000 grant to get started and got $20,000 more the next year from the local district superintendent's office. Do not forget to ask others who are in charge of finances outside of your congregation if they would be willing to support what you are doing to build the Kingdom of God.

One last example: when our staff finished reading *Simple Church* by Thom Rainer and Eric Geiger, we began realizing that some of our ministries had ballooned beyond the mission or vision of the church. One area was our missions budget. We were supporting 27 different missions and missionaries during those early years. And while that might sound grand, the problem was we did not have a relationship with most of them and only a few allowed us the ability to align our mission and vision with theirs. So, we began the hard work of reallocating funds. As missionaries would retire we would move their support monies over to the remaining missionaries who were still active. Eventually we got down to one couple who work for Wycliffe in South East Asia and who have a strong relationship with our church and our mission/vision. We also cut some of our local missions funding so that we could pour more support into our food pantry, clothing pantry, and new campuses. These ministries are aligned with our mission and vision and they give our members a chance to put their faith into action in a real and personal way.

We also made the decision that we needed to commit to one place globally where we could make a massive investment in an effort to make substantial change for the people there. We made the call to work solely in one village in Sierra Leone, West Africa where a 10-year war had left the country torn and broken. We sent small teams of leaders to the village of Maboleh, Sierra Leone where they discovered that the basics of food, water and hygiene were the places we needed to start. Since then I have been there five times myself. One of those trips was when we dedicated the new church building in our sister village. I also addressed the entire annual conference of the United Methodist Church in Sierra Leone that year as a way to encourage them and to show signs of our commitment to support them.

Reflection Questions:

+ What are the ministries that are happening at your church just because we've always done them but they have little to no impact on the mission and vision God has given your church?

+ What is your yearly budget process? How can it be realigned so that it supports the mission and vision?

+ What are the areas of your current budget that need to be reallocated?

+ What is the missional focus of your congregation? What would it take to boil it down and intensify it so that it has more impact?

Chapter 6
Recruiting the Launch Team

Okay, you've evaluated your brains out. You have taken the hard steps of cutting back, cutting out or maybe even letting go. You are either worn out and ready for a nap or you are totally energized and jumping out of your skin and ready to get started. Do not start anything yet! That was one of my mistakes. I am an off the chart optimist and that means that all I need is to see a little bit of movement and I will think we're ready to go to the next step. If I have not said it yet, I will say it here: having a great team around you is a non-negotiable. I have been abundantly blessed to have great people around me who love Jesus and His Church. They also love me and they took time to get to know my heart, how I process information, to learn to not take me seriously until I have said it three times, and to let me ramble until the whole picture was out of my head.

I am also blessed that they call me out when my shortcomings start showing up to derail the party. They are the people who told me it would take six months when I thought it would take six weeks. They are also the people who told me it would take more money than I thought it would or should take. I love those kind of people...and so should you. Make sure you have some people like that around you, you are going to need them. They will support you and call you out and you need both.

I am a motivator, and inspirer, and an action person. I recently had someone tell me that I could sell a used car to a used car salesman.

I am pretty sure he meant that in a good way since it was the morning we launched our most recent capital campaign. Personality indicators tell me all the things I know about myself. On the Myers-Briggs scale I am and ENFP which means I'm creative and impulsive, extroverted and highly feeling of other people's emotions. On the DISC inventory I am a strong "I" with a "D" in second place. I know all those things about myself because as a team we take the time necessary to find those things out about ourselves and each other. If there is one thing that can totally wreck God's vision for your church, it is a team that does not get along because they do not understand the personality dynamics that exist in themselves and the other team members that they work with. When we experience change in our team members (it happens, get ready for it now so that it does not floor you when it happens) we schedule a team retreat and book an expert that will walk us through one of any number of personality indicators that are on the market.

We have used Strength Finders, Myers-Briggs, DISC Inventory, and Spiritual Gift Inventories. These are all personality and work style indicators that can help people understand who they are. These tools have also helped us understand why people we work with on our staff operate the way they do. This has been so important to us that we budgeted for a trained expert in the field to guide us through the day a way so that all of us could participate. That was something we learned the hard way. We allowed one of the staff members to facilitate once and none of us got to know that person and they felt left out… not good, do not do it. So, bite the bullet and hire someone. Remember to check around in the congregation to make sure there isn't an expert sitting in one of the seats each weekend.

> **Not listening to someone else who has something from God that will help you successfully negotiate the change is not just ill-advised, it's sinful.**

Let me just stop here for a moment and say something that may be obvious that I don't want you to miss it. If you have not figured it out by now, one of things that we have done constantly is to use the resources of God's Kingdom to help us navigate the waves of change. I have mentioned a bunch of different things we have done in the area of resourcing: people, books, professionals, coaches, mentors, other churches, friends, experts from within our congregation who work in a coinciding field, denominational leaders, non-denominational leaders, conferences, and the list goes on.

Do not think you have to do this on your own. As a matter of fact, I would say to you that if it is truly a significant and God-given transformation that you and your church have been called to, then you cannot do it on your own and if you try, it will fail. I am a firm believer in the Kingdom of God and that God uses each of us to accomplish His work. Not listening to someone else who has something from God that will help you successfully negotiate the change God has called you to is not just ill-advised, it is sinful. If God has someone right in front of me who knows more than I do I have learned to trust that maybe, just maybe they are there because God sent them. I have no interest in re-creating the wheel if someone has already been there.

Alright, back to moving on to the next level. When God called us to a new thing it was a new church start. That call led us to being a multi-site church because that's what we believe God was directing us to become. So, I am going to tell you what we did next. But if you have been called to some other kind of transformation that may mean launching a contemporary service, moving from an inward to an outward focused church (Ed Stetzer's work is valuable in this area), or starting a new ministry that has been identified as a need in your community, please keep reading. Many of the things we did relate to any kind of change or new start.

After, and **only** after, (did I say that with enough emphasis?) we heard from God, crafted a clear mission and vision for the church, prayed and fasted, consulted, reworked the budget, and introduced the plan to the congregation was it time for us to get things started. The first step we took was to identify the campus pastor. In your ministry start up or transformation it may mean you need to identify who the leader will be. I can tell you that if you're the pastor, it is most likely not you. Even without knowing your context or environment I can say with a pretty strong sense of certainty that it's not going to be you. You need to lead everyone from the top and you cannot take on the project and lead at the same time. Make sense? Good, let's move on.

The first thing you need to do in finding the right person is to know what you want the person to do. Your team will need to draw up a job description for the leader you are looking for. It is like looking for an arrow only after you know what the target is. Do not get this backwards. A lot of churches go looking for a person to lead a ministry or to be a staff member or even a pastor without really knowing what they are looking for. Here is a resource you are going to want to plug into: The Vanderbloemen Search Group. They have all kinds of free resources that can help churches figure out what they need. They also have an excellent podcast that I listen to all the time via my Stitcher app. If that doesn't work you can go so far as to hire them to find the right fit for your church. Again, I said it earlier, I will say it again, do not go it alone. Use the resources that are out there. God has blessed these people with some very specific skills to help churches like yours go through the change He has called you to. Think of it this way…God trained up someone in a specialized way and then called you and your church to change, knowing that He already had the right person/people trained and standing by. Do not make God smack His forehead with the palm of His hand, okay?

> "The first thing you need to do in finding the right person is knowing what you want the person to do."

> Vanderbloemen Search Group.
> www.vanderbloemen.com

At CrossPoint, we have gotten into the groove of doing national searches for personnel alongside of our local advertising. We go outside of our denomination because we believe finding the right person is up to God so we cast a wide net. We also go outside of our denomination because honestly, there are some non-denominational churches who are knocking it out of the park and we want that kind of knowledge, experience, and potential. You will need to carve out the time needed to interview. You will need to create an interview team. It would not surprise me if you do not already have someone in your congregation who is good at interviewing as a part of their job. Because of that, they have the skills the church needs to help find the right person. Ask that person to be on the team.

For us, our executive pastor, our chair of staff/parish relations committee, and our operations manager all have those skills. We also bring in a person who has expertise in the field of interviewing to be a part of the process. We do phone interviews, then in-person interviews, and finally I sit down with them to see if they're the right fit for us. By this point the team has vetted out the applicants and I'm seeing their top picks. This all costs some money so you'll need to budget for change by making sure you have the financial resources set aside to advertise, interview, buy supper, and maybe even put a candidate up in a hotel overnight.

At CrossPoint, we are clear on what we are looking for. We need to see a love for God that shines through, as well as skills for the job, personality, energy, enthusiasm, an ability to communicate clearly, and a love for what we're asking them to do. We ask about their personality type information like Myers-Briggs or DISC or Strength Finders. If they do not know their personality type, we give them some ways they can tells us about themselves that help us understand who they are: introvert or extrovert, processer or knee jerk, etc.

Hiring is important so we take our time and do our homework. We check the internet for crazy things that might be on Facebook or Instagram. We call references. We pray. And sometimes we stop the process and start over. This is too important to mess up…and man have we messed up. When we (I really mean I) rush things it has almost always ended up going sideways or south. We have hired several campus pastors who only lasted a year. Each one was for very different reasons, none of which we saw in the interviews. Our last few hires have been good because we took the time necessary to find the right persons.

The next hire for a multi-site launch is the worship leader. We start our campuses with a part time worship leader who is responsible for practicing with the band, recruiting new band members, leading on Sunday mornings, and choosing the music at their campus. This means an average of 10-12 hours a week. This position is almost as important as the campus pastor because of the impact music has on people. The right environment, the best preaching, a great children's ministry can all be undone by a mediocre worship set. Once again, we throw as wide of a net as we can in order to find the right person.

We are fortunate that we have been around for a while and have built a reputation for great worship that people want to come and work for us. That was not true at first. We had to look everywhere to find the right people. We also trusted that God had called us to do this so God was going to bring the right person to our door. That has happened several times and it never ceases to amaze me. The worship leader at our South Hanover campus bumped into me while I was sitting at a Starbucks. Our God is so very good. Once the worship leader is on board we help him/her find the people who will make up the band. Usually a good musician will bring some people with them. And while they may not be in the same spiritual condition the worship leader is in, our door is open to what God can do in the life of a person who is willing to get up on a Sunday morning and play at a church.

With the momentum of having the campus pastor and worship leader chosen we can start working on the leadership team. The campus leaders are those who lead the children's ministry, youth ministry, hospitality teams, setup/tear down teams, etc. These are extremely vital positions that need to be filled by people who love Jesus, love your church and are self-starters. They also need to be people who can work well as a part of a team...no Lone Rangers. To find those people you need to first establish the positions that needed filled. What I mean is, what are you going to do first?

Most churches launch a ministry and then build it while it is in the air. With the campus pastor and worship leader on board you will need to decide what else you want to do and benchmarks for when you do them. Let me tell you what I have heard loud and clear from all the resources I use: make sure you have got children's ministry people on board early. You don't want to mess up the care of children and families. They will often be the way your church starts and the way your ministry grows. Families tell other families when they find the right place. You may want to go so far as to make this a paid position early on to ensure that it's high enough on the priority list.

Let me take a moment right here to address something that we did not see coming...team burn-out. The startup team for any ministry will often give all they have each weekend. That means they are setting up, tearing down, manning the ship and loading the guns (so to speak). Eventually that team of people will start feeling tired and worn out. It is important to make sure that the campus pastor knows how to recognize the signs of burn-out and to be proactive by giving people a Sunday off – on purpose, for no other reason than to just have them sit in on a Sunday morning with no responsibilities. By doing so the person gets spiritually refreshed, reenergized and may even see things that need fixed or can be improved upon when they return the next week. It is a win-win all around.

We discovered that everyone started frying about one year to 18 months into the first launch. We needed to give them a break and, at the same time, celebrate them while re-establishing the vision. We called everyone together, celebrated an anniversary, thanked the volunteers, and recast the vision for the campus. We then took on the task of finding people who could shadow those in charge and then started a schedule that rotated people in and out. Everyone was happy and the campus got a shot in the arm at the same time. We didn't do it perfectly and we missed a few people who told us they were fine, but they were not. In a "do over" I would make everyone find a shadow.

This is Going to Affect Everyone

One last thing before we move on to the non-negotiables for change. While there are several things I wish I could go back and do differently, there is one thing that stands out the most. While we had done a good bit of preparation for the change to come, I did not anticipate the level of impact that moving from mainline to multi-site would have on the first campus. Consequently, we (especially me) did not do a good job

> If I could, I would go back and develop an entire congregational care ministry...

of caring for the people who were the long-time members of the church. If I could, I would go back and develop an entire congregational care ministry that would have assured the kind of care for our members that every church should be offering. I dove so fully into the new start that I found it difficult to look back at those who needed their pastor.

Admittedly, I had high expectations of a congregation that had gone through so much preparation. Purpose Driven this and 40 days of that was not enough to prepare everyone for the coming changes. I could not let go and throw myself headlong into the launch of the new campuses without the detriment of those who were at the first campus. Even worse, when people tried to tell me what was happening I practically refused to listen. In my mind, we were advancing the Kingdom. What better task is there that should cause everyone to want to give as much as the leader is giving. I expected everyone to be with me in the new adventure, they were not. And because of that they were looking for me to care for their needs when all I wanted to do was build God's Kingdom. I blame some of it on the fact that I was a sergeant in the U.S. Marine Corps. Oh, how I have repented of that.

The biggest mistake we made that led to this issue is contained in just a few but noteworthy words. We had allowed people to say, "hey pastor, you can do whatever you like, as long as it doesn't affect me." What they were saying is, as long as it doesn't affect the service I go to, as long as it doesn't affect what songs I sing, as long as it doesn't mess with worship times on Sunday morning, as long as I get the care and service I need – when I need it. Hear me when I say that it was wrong for us to allow people to say that. Whatever the church does affects all of the church. No one is protected from change, as much as we would like to be.

Most people don't like change, but if God calls your church to change in some way, it WILL affect everyone, it SHOULD affect everyone. If nothing more it should affect their prayer life. Everyone should be praying for the new thing God has called you to. It will affect resources, finances, pastoral availability, programmatic ministries. In fact, it will have an effect on everything the church is currently doing. If it does not have that kind of systemic effect, then you haven't shared the vision widely enough yet. Everyone needs to know how this new adventure you are on will affect them. For some, they need to know because they are not sure they want to stick around. For others, they need to know because they are anticipating being a part of it. Either way, it will affect everyone in some way. Make sure you let them know that or they will come back later and remind you that you said it wouldn't affect them and now it is affecting them and you'll be the bad guy. And it can get ugly real fast.

Reflection Questions:

+ What resources might be available to you and the congregation to help you navigate the change God is calling you to?
+ If you do not have job descriptions for all of your staff positions (paid and unpaid) it's time to create them. How can you create useful job descriptions for every position at your church?
+ Which persons from within your current staff or congregation who might be able to fill the needed positions? Who can help you with this?
+ What can you do to help everyone be a part of the change?

Chapter 7
The Non-negotiables for Change

In every move of God there are certain things that will need to be a part of that move. I mentioned one of these in the previous chapter: having a great team around you is a must. Great teams do great things. I have one of the best teams in the world around me. They offer me insight, direction, passion, balance and so much more. This is covered in chapter four. Let me just add this one vital piece to the staffing component: make sure they are team players. The staff (paid or volunteer) need to be working together to accomplish the mission and vision of the church. Lone Rangers do not bring healthy, long term transformation. It's too easy to get siloed in ministry – team players, by their nature, will work against siloing.

So, what are some of the other non-negotiables that you will need to have as you catch the wave God has sent your way? Here are some of the things we did that, as I look back, made all the difference in the world.

Prayer Changes Everything

This first one on my list might seem like a no brainer but it is surprising how many times we forgot about its' importance. Prayer is the breath of life and, just like air, we cannot live without it. It is the same when any kind of significant change is called for by God upon leaders and churches. We cannot survive or successfully navigate any change without prayer. I believe that most likely it was through prayer that you received the stirrings in your heart that some kind of change was needed. You felt the wave beginning to form as God spoke to you while in one of those deeper moments of prayer that you take from time to time. For me, it is while I'm out on my bicycle. God and I seem to have these amazing talks while I'm just riding along, peddling to a song in my head.

It is prayer that led you here and it is prayer that will see you through it. God has a plan for you and your church and the best way to make sure that plan is done the way God wants it done is to be in constant conversation with the designer of the plan. We have had some construction projects happen around the church over the years. One of the most important aspects of all those projects has been communication. We are blessed at CrossPoint Church to have Bill. He is a member of the church and he has been instrumental in every project. He is the guy who communicates back and forth with the contractors about what the church wants. He takes time to capture the vision of the project and then sees it through to the end, constantly communicating with me, our office, and the contractors. Without Bill communicating and checking in on things, the projects we've had could have gone woefully off course. There were some pretty close calls when Bill found that something had been started that would have disrupted the entire plan down the road. Bill would call me and call the contractor and consult the drawings and get things corrected. Thank God for Bill.

I tell you all of this about Bill to emphasis my point…God is directing the transformation of your church. **Make sure you are in constant communication with God so that the plan does not go off course.** It is so easy to want to sit back and allow the plan to function on auto-pilot, especially when you have worn yourself out doing all the things that change requires. All those

> And I tell you that you are Peter, and on this rock I will build my church…
> Matthew 16:18 NIV

meeting, all the conversations, all the documents, all of the financial numbers, all the sleepless nights – all of those things can convince you that the change God is asking of you and your church are up to you. They are not. Jesus said clearly that He is in charge of building His church, not us. Jesus is the one in charge of the transformation and the building of the new thing He is doing. Our obedience to the direction of Jesus requires an ever-constant line of communication through prayer.

Here are a few things we did. As the vision pastor of CrossPoint Church I met every other week with a personal prayer partner with whom I maintained an accountability relationship. Bob and I met to talk about life and the things that were going on and then we would pray for each other. We also committed to praying for each other every day, as well as praying through especially difficult times. Bob would also be sure to pray for me when I traveled, when I had an important meeting to go to, and even when I was on vacation. I also met with Steve every Sunday morning for an entire year prior to the launch of our second and third campuses. Steve would come in early to meet with me before anyone else got to the church. We would get caught up on where things were and then we'd pray. Steve was not only materially invested in the new start but, he was also spiritually invested. As a matter of fact, Steve is still there and still a part of the prayer team for the campus he and his family attend.

We asked all our small groups to be in prayer for the transitions that were happening. Small groups are places where people get a chance to talk about the things that are happening at their church. What better place for people to also be praying? Prayer changes things and our small group prayers did great things to open doors, soften hearts, heal wounds, and lift-up the body.

In many of our meetings we would face difficult decisions. We may not have known that the decision was going to happen at that meeting but God did. We were pretty good at recognizing when things were getting tense or intense. At that point we would call the meeting to a halt so that we could pray for God's direction. There were many occasions when those prayers changed the atmosphere and moved us forward. Our staff modeled that willingness to stop and pray at our meetings. There were more than a few times when we would stop and ask everyone to leave the tables in order to pray. When we returned, we would ask everyone to share what they heard from God. In those moments, we not only felt God's presence in mighty ways, we also understood God's leading with new clarity.

Thom Rainer points out in his newest book, *Who Moved My Pulpit*, that prayer changes people who are struggling, it softens the hard hearts of those who are opposed to the changes, it heals the broken hearts of those who feel they are losing something because of the changes, and it makes a way for conversations between those who otherwise do not want to speak to each other. I will never forget praying with the two older members of our congregation who were taking pictures of the front of the sanctuary at our first campus the week before we tore out the 90-year-old pulpit, lectern, choir loft, and organ to make way for a new stage style platform for worship. The one lady had tears running down her face as she stated that it will never look this way again. She was right. But, through prayer, we remained a church together and those ladies are still a part of the worshippers at that campus. I could not see the changes through their eyes. However, through prayer we could cry together and look forward

> And we know that in all things God works for the good of those who love Him, who have been called according to His purpose.
> Romans 8:28 NIV

together in hopes that everything God was doing would work for the good for those who love Him and who are called, according to His purposes.

Prayer makes things possible. So, we started a prayer group who committed to praying through the transition. This was a temporary group who met together for the specific purpose of praying for the transition. They did not all meet together physically, but they all committed to prayer. They received regular updates on how things were going. Their prayers were powerful tools, especially in the spiritual battles that change can create.

Now, before you think that this all sounds wonderful, there were lots of times when we messed this up. There were times when we finished meetings and looked at each other and said, "we forgot to pray." There were times when we forgot to communicate with our prayer team. There were times when we should have called everyone to a time of prayer and fasting and we were so focused on what was happening or what we were going to say that we forgot to ask everyone to pray first. When we did pray, things went better. When we forgot to pray, things usually didn't go as well as they could have. God is gracious and gave us a lot of room when we failed, but it could have gone better if we would have prayed first. There is a New Testament process for launching a new thing, it must happen with prayer and fasting.

> *Paul and Barnabas appointed elders for them in each church and, with prayer and fasting, committed them to the Lord, in whom they had put their trust.*
> **Acts 14:23 NIV**

Mentors For Everyone

There are just some things that only certain people can say to you. There are things your spouse can say to you that no one else can say. There are things that a close friend can say that no one else can say. All of this is because there has been a permission giving that has taken place. Through the vows of marriage, you gave the other person permission to tell you the truth about yourself. Through the bond of friendship, you have given that other person the privilege of saying what's on their mind about how you act or what you have said.

Mentors are those people who have been through what we are going through and can help us manage the churning waters. They are wise because they have been there. They are compassionate because they know the pain and the passion. They have listening ears because someone once listened to them. They offer direction because they are in tune with what God wants for you and your church. Mentors are those people who can challenge us to the core of our souls because

71

they know us well and we have given them the right to speak the truth. My mentor was, and still is, Ted. He is a saint to me. He and I are cut from the same cloth so he knows my heart, my mind and my desires. He also pastored the first campus (CrossPoint @Colonial Park) for 12 years prior to my arrival and he knows the people who are there. I knew that if we were going to survive the kinds of changes God was calling us to that I would need his guidance and wisdom.

Ted and I met once a month to talk out things that I was going through. The meetings were about me, not him. We talked about where things were at that moment and about the difficult things that were happening. We talked about the unexpected things. We talked about spiritual things. We talked about this book. It was Ted who told me to stop writing and just live it for a while. He wisely told me that there were more things coming that we needed to live through before I could write this book...and he was right.

Because of the significant things that came up while Ted and I met I asked that everyone on our staff find a mentor. I made it a requirement that everyone find someone who was in a place where they could speak guidance, wisdom and truth to their souls. It was a bit uncomfortable because not everyone wanted to bear their souls like that to another person. Other's did not have the kinds of spiritual connections with others that are necessary to allow them to find a mentor. By the way, that is an indicator that the person may not be the right person on the bus. Everyone got a mentor of some kind and it was so very helpful to each of us individually that it became one of my requirements for our staff.

Coaches for Everyone

When we first began the process of change we were given a requirement by our denominational leaders: get a coach who will help you through the transitions. It was a new concept for us and so we were a bit gun shy on the whole

Coaching4Clergy at:
www.coaching4clergy.com

idea. We knew what the word meant in the sports world but what did it mean in the church/leadership world? So, we found a guy named Val Hastings who runs a coaching firm called, you ready for this, Coaching4Clergy. Val is a great coach and I highly recommend him and his group of coaches. I remember the first session with Val. Although he was just getting to know me he had the ability to set me at ease and guide my mind toward really thinking things out loud – that was incredibly helpful. We also brought Val in for some of our team coaching sessions when we knew we were not getting along or that we had hit a personality issue and we needed help. The first-time Val came in we were in pretty rough shape. He told us we needed a psychologist, not a coach. Everyone in the room laughed except Val… he was right.

I remember my second meeting with him. He asked me a question that he would ask at key moments through the process. At a poignant moment in the conversation where I was hesitating to give an answer he asked: "what are you afraid of?" Wow, I did not see that coming. I wasn't ready for someone to ask such a pointed and exact question. It cut through all the garbage and got to the heart of the matter in a split second. I was afraid of something, he knew it, and his job was to help me know it too. From then on, I knew this was going to be worth every penny. Yes, coaching cost some serious money but, it is worth it. Make sure you budget some of your personal funds as well as some of the churches monies toward coaching. Personal because you are going to discover you will want to talk to your coach about how you are doing and where you are going personally.

You also need funds that can be used specifically for the work that you and the staff are doing. A coach can bring clarity and direction, but the best thing a good coach does is help you see what you need to do and then sends you back out into the game. We do not see coaching as an option; for us it is a necessity that makes a huge difference for me, our team, and the church, as a whole. This is so crucial that our executive pastor has gone on to get a certification in coaching, all our staff go to Coaching4Clergy's introductory courses, we teach coaching techniques to our leaders, and we have coaching as one of modes of operation at every level of leadership.

Listening to everyone

I stated earlier just how important communication is to the transformation process. Being able to speak and listen is what communication is all about. We know that however, as church leaders we tend to rely on our speaking skills more than our listening skills. People in your church want and need to be heard. In some systems, the pastor is a temporary assignment and the people feel that they were here before you and they will be here after you. Because it is their church, leaders need to be spending time listening to how the congregation is feeling and thinking. So, we started doing something we called "listening sessions." They are (we still do them from time to time) opportunities for the pastors and/or staff to sit down with a group of people and hear what is on the minds of those who sit in the seats each week.

We do these gatherings in homes, at the church, in the evenings, on Sunday afternoons, on weekday afternoons, when a small group invites us and at any other time we think that it is convenient for people to attend. We attempt to keep them small, 10-20 at most. Our goal is to allow space for everyone who attends to be able to speak, no matter what it is they need to say. We try hard to let everyone know that it's okay to have a difference of opinion or to disagree openly. Admittedly, that is not an easy thing to do for most of us. We live in a world where what you say can and will be used against you when needed. Yet we believe that it is better to do life together, and that means speaking openly and honestly with each other.

Dealing with Dissenters

One of the jobs of every pastor and church is to help people have a dynamic relationship with Jesus and to be all that God has created and called them to be. Some of those who sit in the seats of a church will balk at this notion. They may not want to be closer to Jesus or they already feel close enough. There are some who believe that they have already reached the highest height of spirituality and are therefore uniquely positioned to advise and direct the rest of the church and the pastor on how things should be done. In most cases, these persons become problematic, often they did not want to be a part of the process. They simply wanted to proclaim what they thought was best without being a part of the systems or processes that affect the needed changes. These people may believe that the changes you are tying to institute are wrong for the church and may even quote scripture to advance their argument.

If left alone, these persons can become divisive dissenters within the body. Like a bad infection, they will need to be cared for before they develop into something life threatening. We practice a method that we believe is clearly outlined in Matthew 18:15-17:

> [15]If your brother sins against you, go and show him his fault, just between the two of you. If he listens to you, you have won your brother over. [16]But if he will not listen, take one or two others along, so that 'every matter may be established by the testimony of two or three witnesses.' [17]If he refuses to listen to them, tell it to the church; and if he refuses to listen even to the church, treat him as you would a pagan or a tax collector. (NIV)

We believe this passage helps us walk through a process where we can biblically confront someone who is in direct opposition to what God is telling the church to do. Now, notice, this is a process. It is not a once and over kind of thing. Also, this must be done in Christian love, not with a desire to rebuke or correct or get the person in line. I have seen too many good church members who disagreed with the direction of the church be hurt by those who did not use this method with love and grace. Also, notice that the passage makes clear that the persons who are causing the difficulties are not expelled from the fellowship. Instead they are treated as those who do not understand (pagans and tax collectors). That means they were treated with love, respect, understanding, grace, and patience.

Now, I say all of that with the understanding that there are those who might continue to just be dissenters. They are convinced that they know what is best for the church, not you, and their job is to take you to school, so it seems. We have had a few of these kinds of people at CrossPoint Church over the years. As the vision pastor I followed Matthew 18 and, when all else failed and after a great deal of prayer, I encouraged them to find a church that aligned with what they believed should be happening. There are lots of churches in the world, why stay at one with whom you disagree, right? And why should the whole church suffer at the hands of a vocal dissenter?

I still recall the day I invited one of these persons into my office. Pastor Jen, our executive pastor, was with me that day as a part of our way of living out Matthew 18. I invited the dissenter to tell me all that he believed we should be doing. It was no different than what I have been hearing from him for quite some time. He had not changed his beliefs about what we should do. After much prayer about his recommendations, we were not going to change our plan either. He was visibly upset by this because he believed he was right. During the conversation, we discussed over and over how we differed. I finally said to him what I believe God told me to say (you can differ with me if you like): he had become like a "seed under my dentures and it was time for him to find another church." Now, let me clear the record, I do not wear dentures but, the metaphor worked. He sat back, paused for a moment, sat forward again and said: you're right, thank you, it is time for me to go. We ended with a hug and with blessings on each other. Staying true to what God has given you is a non-negotiable and that means there will be those who will need to go to make room for those who are coming because of the change.

Have Fun

This is great way to end this chapter. When I was a young boy my family went to church every Sunday. It was a small town, Evangelical United Brethren church in rural Pennsylvania. It was very traditional. I was what would later be diagnosed as Attention Deficit Hyperactivity Disorder (ADHD). My family just called it "fidgety." I did not sit still for long. It was difficult for me to focus on one thing at a time, I was easily distracted, and church services at my traditional, small town church were an endurance test at best, and excruciating at worst. I did my best and my mother, God bless her for all I put her through, did her best to keep me occupied. When I got out of control I would get pinched on the leg. When I got older, in an effort to keep me engaged and make the time go by, my mother would take notes and then ask me questions at lunch time. Outside of the social factors of gathering with friends and seeing girls I liked, Sunday's were agony for me.

> I remember at that young age, with my fist clenched, that if I were in charge of church, it would be fun.

At a young age, I knew that something needed to change for kids like me. I still find it amazing that I did not leave the church for good based on most churches' inability to meet the needs of its attenders who struggle. Instead, I remember saying at that young age, with my fist clenched, that if I were in charge of church, it would be fun. As an adult, as a pastor, and as one of the people in charge of the direction of our church, I have continued to make sure we make it fun. Our children's areas are brightly decorated, our meetings have loads of laughter, and each new staff person receives a NERF gun to defend themselves because we all have them and we know how to use them.

Someone on staff recently relayed his feelings to another person about how we connect and have fun together by saying: we take what we do and why we do it very seriously, we do not take ourselves seriously at all. We laugh together, we buy gifts for each other, we play jokes on each other, we have pet names for each other, we eat meals together, and we enjoy life together – with a lot of laughter mixed in. In short, we have fun. What you are doing in transforming a church is vitally important to the Kingdom of God and people you will reach. But, do not get so caught up in the seriousness that you forget that God also gave us laughter and fun.

Reflection Questions:

+ What is the current look and condition of your prayer ministries?
+ What will you need to do to get prayer to a level where it is primary to the change?
+ Are there mentors and coaches you can call upon to help you process the changes?
+ How do you deal with dissention? How do you develop a policy that effectively deals with dissention with grace and love?
+ How is fun and laughter incorporated into the life of your congregation?

Chapter 8
Shift to Discipleship

The whole process of change is an exercise in discipleship. Change will either grow you or leave you lying lifeless on the beach. Change will either push you further into a place of dependency on God or make you turn away. Change will drive you deeper into the Bible or make you close the book thinking that what it says is madness. All of these things are aspects of discipleship. All of them are things we may (I say must) go through to be more faithful followers of Jesus. The challenge of change in the life of a congregation will reveal the spiritual needs of the people who attend that church. You must do as much as you possibly can to prepare the congregation knowing that there will be those who you thought were ready but, were not. They may have been Sunday morning group teachers, small group leaders, hospitality team leaders, board members, and even staff members.

As a church, we spent years getting ready for change. We did congregation-wide studies that included preaching series and corresponding small group studies, Disciple Bible courses, Steven's Ministry, small group leaders training, conferences, planning retreats, church council retreats, days apart, joint book studies for staff and leaders, and more. We did it all. And when the changes started hitting us, there were many who were ready. And there were some surprises. There were some leaders who refused to read the first line of Purpose Driven Church by Rick Warren where it clearly states, *It's not about you.* We heard from those who were not ready when they thought that our church was already big enough or that dividing our resources to launch new sites and reach new people was too risky. Some of those people left…most stayed, thank God. It's not been easy. I can say that those who stayed, developed a faith that can be challenged but not destroyed. They are stronger and more courageous than ever before.

What that told us, along with every growth and discipleship guru out there, was this; a discipleship process is a must. So, we went about developing a life development process that fits into our theme of threes. We reduced our plan down to three easy words: Grow, Give, and Lead. It is our desire to see each person grow in the faith in God, grow in the understanding of who God is, and grow spiritually as they learn who Jesus is. We also want people to learn how to give. As a church that believes strongly in mission work, we encourage greater levels of discipleship by challenging people to give of their very best, to go on mission trips, to develop the habit of tithing, to be generous with what they have and to give by serving others as modeled by Jesus. The last area is an expectation that followers of Jesus will lead others to Him. It is important that the church raise up leaders who are pointing others in the way of following Jesus. These people lead worship, lead studies, lead small groups, lead ministry teams and mission trips, and these are the people who lead our decision-making bodies.

Disciple making is a process and we have developed a progression that looks familiar to most of us. We use the *Grow, Give, Lead* labels to denote the development process much like you find at a college. The *Grow* level is the easiest and is meant for the entry level person who is just starting out their journey with Jesus. This first step primarily concerns itself with the entry level part of our plan. Included at this level is our Foundations class that covers the basics of the faith. It also covers who we are as a church meaning things like our mission, vision, history, core values, and processes. This is the level where people get started. Each class setting functions like a small group so that people get a feel for what a small group is like.

The *Give* level takes what people have learned at the *Grow* level and builds on it with a focus on giving back. The *GIVE* part of our plan helps people learn how to be a giver, according to what the Bible says and in all the ways God has created them to be. Here people learn the important skills they need to have to become the leaders God wants them to be. Folks also learn what is means to become a member of CrossPoint Church as well as how they can get involved. To facilitate that we teach a class at the 200 level on spiritual gifts and how those gifts and your personal gift mix will best fit a particular ministry.

The *Lead* level is where we teach leadership development and includes our leadership institute section. This is where we offer leadership training and offer leadership practicums. We engage in shadowing, mentoring and coaching at this level. Leaders are encouraged to step into opportunities where they can shine with a safety net in case they crash and burn. At the *Lead* level the group gets smaller but a whole lot more intense. The challenge for many people is saying no so that they can focus in on what God wants them to do.

The process of purposefully training up the people of God is vital for the changes that God is planning for your church. People will need to learn new things as a part of the transformation process or they will get left behind. People will need to keep learning or the changes may not make sense. People need to learn because when God starts changing a church He also starts changing hearts and minds. People will need a place where they will learn about the new things God is doing in their lives.

Reflection Questions:

+ What effective and thorough discipleship plan is currently in place that is in line with your mission and vision?
+ How is your discipleship plan easy to step into and easy to use?
+ Who are the persons who are currently leading at a high level of discipleship that you can leverage toward the changes?

Chapter 9
Stay the Course

There's one more thing I wanted to say. Finally, stay the course. One of my favorite movies of all time is *The Patriot*, with Mel Gibson. While the movie is not historically accurate, it is still a great drama about a time-period I really enjoy. In this movie, the main character, played by Gibson, meets defeat after damaging defeat. After losing two children, his home, and his fortune he is ready to give up, to throw in the towel and allow the British to win the American Revolution. His commanding officer reminds him of the importance of staying the course, that none of the things that have happened can be surrendered to a lost hope or spirit. The speech gets him back on his feet and drives him to lead his men to victory over the mighty British army.

I want to say the same thing to you. When you are going through a time of transformation personally, or with your church, stay the course. If it has gotten difficult, challenging and heartbreaking, stay the course. If there are moments when you feel like you have lost everything, including your sanity, stay the course. The old statement that says: *if God brought you to it, He'll see you through it*, is passé and even a bit corny. It is biblically accurate and there are more than a few pastors and church leaders who could testify to its truth.

> ...being confident of this, that he who began a good work in you will carry it on to completion until the day of Christ Jesus.
> **Philippians 1:6 NIV**

Staying the course is challenging...so much so that our staff adopted it as a part of a one-year plan several years into the transition. We had found ourselves in a place where we were advancing the transitions that were needed on a slow and steady course so that every three to six months we were introducing the next phase. Now that does not sound bad until you throw in all the other things that go along with change that I have mentioned before such as: people leaving, listening sessions, retreats and planning meetings, and more. We went to our coming year planning retreat and everyone was exhausted. So, we said that we were going to work into next year's plan an element of "trudging." Now you may have reacted to that word like I did at first...I had to look it up. The last place I heard the word used was in the movie *A Knights Tale* where Paul Bettany was portraying Henry Chaucer who proclaimed, as he walked down the road, that he was "trudging." It means: *to walk slowly and with heavy steps, typically because of exhaustion or harsh conditions, a difficult or laborious walk.* That was us at one point...all we had left was trudging, so we committed to trudging. Not that we did nothing, you're still moving things forward when your trudging. It is just that it looks like those guys at the top of Mount Everest. They use breathing apparatus, and spikes on their boots, and its 20 below, and the wind is blasting them. Every step requires great labor, they are trudging.

We knew that we were not far from the top of the hill. We knew that what God started God would finish. We knew that walking would be laborious. In spite of it all, we chose to stay the course and keep walking. There were days when it felt like we were moving through the stickiest, deepest mud on earth. There were other days when it felt like the burden was light and the weight was easy. There were days when we got encouragement from congregational members and there were days when the encouragement came from the outside looking in.

A close friend, who is not only a denominational leader but someone who knows our church and staff, told me that any church going through all of the changes that we went through: death of a beloved senior pastor, change in leadership structure and style, change in church name, change in the vision, launching two new campuses, reworking the front of the sanctuary into a more modern platform, moving the worship times, realigning staff; any one of them is enough to close a church. We navigated no less than eight major changes in five years. To the credit of the members of CrossPoint Church, we only lost 15% of the congregation through the changes. We have finally gotten back to where we were when we started all of this and we have gotten a whole new momentum that is pushing us into a fourth campus. It's exciting to see what God is going to do next.

Now, hear this loud and clear…this was no overnight success nor is God done yet. We did a series of messages in the summer of 2016 that focused on Joseph and the last 14 chapters of Genesis. Joseph got his dreams about his father Jacob, his mother and his 11 brothers when he is 17 years old (Genesis 37:2). He does not step into the position of leadership that will have his brothers bowing to him until he's 30 years old (Genesis 41:46). He does not realize the full dream until he is at least 39 (Genesis 42:6 and Genesis 45:6). That means he holds onto the dream that is given to him at 17 until he is 39. How many of us are willing to live into a dream for 22 years? God has pieces of the puzzle that you may never see that must be in place before the dream can be realized. God is the only one who has the vantage point from which to see the entire picture. Our task as leaders is to trust the process and believe that God is active and busy building the Kingdom on earth as it is in heaven.

The "take away" for us is that dreams take time to unfold and become realities. It took Joseph a minimum of 22 years before his dream came true. Will you stay the course for as long as God calls you to the dream he's given your church? We are staying the course and I hope you will too. The end is not far away and you will never know when God's going to

> **What good will it be for a man if he gains the whole world, yet forfeits his soul? Or what can a man give in exchange for his soul.**
> **Matthew 16:26 NIV**

show up in ways that will leave your jaw on the floor. I personally believe that is why long term pastorates of essential for congregational transformation.

Now, all that being said, here is a word of caution. The vision God has given you and your church is not worth losing your soul for. Whatever it is that God has asked you (the pastor/leader) or your church (every member) to do, it is sinful to be so myopic that you would burn out, leave the ministry, divorce your spouse, and/or turn your children against the Church and maybe even Jesus. I had to learn that I needed to protect those parts of my life that God gave me to care for. I did not learn it easily and there were times when I had to be told to go home. I also learned that I needed to take time to read books other than church stuff, to go on vacations, to hang out with my three kids (and now their spouses), to love my wife, to chat across the fence with the neighbors, to have a glass of wine with friends, to go hunting, to go to the monastery on retreats, skydive, ride my bicycle, do chores around the house, and basically live a somewhat normal life.

Do not let the work of God destroy your relationship with God or your relationship with others. My wife (Julie) and I still preach that it's God first, then my spouse, then the kids/family, and then the church. It will be easy to get caught up in the work of transforming and changing a church to reach new people and ignite a community with the love of God. Make sure you give some people who are close to you the permission to tell you to go home, to go out on a date, to leave or take the weekend off, to catch a game, or whatever it is that will get your mind off of the church and the work you are doing, even if it is just for a little while.

Reflection Questions:

- What are your own signs of burn out? How have you clearly defined understanding of the balance between faith, family and work?

+ How will you ferret out if there is a willingness on your part and the part of the congregation to stick it out?
+ How do you celebrate the "wins" along the way?
+ You may never personally see the finished product of all your work. How will you long range plan for the future parts of the transformation?

Conclusion

A lot has happened to get me and the church I pastor to this point. As I write this it has been 19 years since I was first appointed to the Colonial Park UMC. It has been 9 years since we launched our second campus and I was reappointed as the vision pastor. There have been earth shattering, bone-jarring things that have happened...not all of them were nice. People can be hard and nasty when they are confronted with change. The unexpected waves can generate feelings in people that are, well, unexpected. If you are the pastor – there are people who will direct their feelings toward you and blame you for all that is happening. It is something people have been doing in churches for a very long time. If you can understand why they are so upset or angry it will be easier to deflect it while all the time praying for them. The executive pastor at CrossPoint, Jen Williams, reminds me that when people lash out, it is hardly ever about what they say it's about. Stay the course with them and you will discover what it's truly about and how you can walk through it together.

I wrote the first five chapters 3 years before I wrote the last four chapters. I wrote the first five and then I felt like I needed to stop. My mentor, Ted, told me to put the book down...that God would tell me when the time was right. I had outlined the remaining 4 chapters, but I had not written them yet. Now was the time. The staff of CrossPoint Church knew it, I knew it, my wife Julie knew it. We all knew it was time.

If you are going to walk a church through the crashing waves of transformational change I can promise you that it will feel like being in huge waves on the beach. They keep pounding and sometimes they feel relentless as you are being tossed around like a rag doll. They can leave you lying in the sand with brush burns and sand in places you don't like to mention. But, when you stand up and brush yourself off you can look around and see the reminders of why you did what you did and why you continue to do what you are doing...because it truly is a beautiful thing God is doing. The church is as beautiful as any beach when it is functioning in the blessings and glory of the Father. The church, with its conglomeration of people, is beautiful when they all sing, loudly, with one voice, that *God's Not Dead* or that *He's a Good, Good Father* or *It Is Well With My Soul*. When a wave comes crashing against you, there remains no doubt that you are alive. Every one of your senses is wakened and it feels so good. And the sun is shining, and the salty sea is leaving its taste in your mouth, and your hair's a bit disheveled, and your legs are a little weak. And you see the next wave, and you pause for a moment and then, with all that God has made you to be, you go running back into the surf to feel it all over again.

May God richly bless you with the pounding of His presence upon your life in such a way that it leaves you wanting more. And so, you go back, again and again...that is what church should be like. Until it is, let us be relentless about making it so.

Printed in the United States
By Bookmasters